always in the kitchen at parties

simple tools for instant CONFIDENCE

Leil Lowndes

Other books by this author:
How to Make Anyone Fall in Love with You
How to Talk to Anyone

HarperElement
An Imprint of HarperCollins*Publishers*
77–85 Fulham Palace Road,
Hammersmith, London W6 8JB

The website address is: www.thorsonselement.com

and *HarperElement* are trademarks of
HarperCollins*Publishers* Ltd

First published in the UK by HarperElement 2006

10 9 8 7 6 5 4 3 2 1

A catalogue record of this book is
available from the British Library

ISBN-13   978-0-00-719978-5
ISBN-10   0-00-719978-3

Printed and bound in Great Britain by
Clays Ltd, St Ives plc

contents

" I used to be very shy. I couldn't look people in the face and became red. I was embarrassed and used to sweat in front of others. Due to low self-esteem and 'slow' self-image, I used to feel inferior to others. But then one day I began to question things. I realized that nobody is better than me. Who told me I'm no good? I realized that the people who make me feel that way are not in that credible or successful a position themselves. So why would I believe what these people say about me? They were not qualified to make such comments. "

TONY V. – SYDNEY, AUSTRALIA

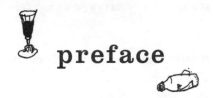

preface

Think back to your grandparents' times, when 'on-line dating' was a twinkle in some yet-unborn techie's eyes, and the words 'pick up' meant 'get your socks off the floor.' If Grandma was always in the kitchen at parties, and Grandpa hid out in the bedroom memorizing guests' coat labels, you wouldn't be here.

Things haven't changed much for those of us who are shy. Well-meaning friends and family still say, 'C'mon, just force yourself to ... go to the party/ask her for a date/talk to him/request a pay rise/join the conversation/speak up at the meeting ...'

Don't they know how hard it is? The anxiety? The wanting to be invisible? The fear you'll say something stupid? The sparkling conversations in your head that you don't have the courage to start? Yet you know you have a lot to offer, and if you could just make eye-contact, speak up and stop hiding out in the kitchen at parties, everything would be OK, and you could get on with your life.

When I was a kid, I had all the usual questions, 'Why is the sky blue?' 'Did Eve have a belly button?' 'What was the best thing *before* sliced bread?'

But 'Why am I shy?' wasn't one of them. I didn't care why. I just wanted a quick cure. However, as a recovered shy, I now realize origins are important. They give you a realistic picture of yourself, what to expect, and how to go about it.

I've heard Shys speculate ...

'It must have been Mum and Dad's fault.'

'Nah, it was those nasty kids in the neighbourhood who called me names.'

'I think it's genetic.'

Actually it can be all of the above. You will discover there are several basic types of Shy. You are either a 'Highly Sensitive Shy' (HSS) who was born with a proclivity towards timidity, or a 'Situational Shy' whose parents and youthful experiences deeply affected you. You could be a little bit of both. Each must have different goals, and each can expect different, but remarkable, results.

The 1940s gave us a gift which saved millions of lives. It is called penicillin. Recent years have given us a gift which can save millions the agony of shyness, which is often called 'Social Anxiety Disorder'. It is not a drug, but it is a formula. It derives from studies on shyness conducted by pioneering researchers in sociology, psychiatry, genetics, biology, physiology and pharmacology. It sounds complicated but I've distilled it down to 66 SHYBUSTERs to cure or curtail your shyness.

I know first-hand how excruciating it is. I used to stand on the sidelines at parties wishing my dress matched the wallpaper to make me invisible. Well into my working years, my face turned into a radish whenever I talked to strangers.

I wish I'd had this book then. I am gratified I can provide it for you now.

A few notes before you start: First, read sequentially through the book so you will understand the significance of each SHYBUSTER. Then, depending on which are most challenging for you personally, you choose the order – easiest to most difficult of course.

Each SHYBUSTER is substantiated by the findings of sociologists and both medical and mental health professionals. If you'd like more information you can go to the original sources, which are referenced in the back of the book. Shyness research is almost synonymous with the names Zimbardo, Carducci, Kagan and a few others. I am grateful to them, and you will find their names many times in the notes.

The stories come from my own stinging shyness and those of Shys I've known. Others come from attendees at my shyness seminars. At first I felt inviting people to a 'Shyness Seminar' would be like telling participants at a 'Fear of Tigers' seminar to meet at the tiger's cage at the zoo. Happily, however, Shys did come and they shared their experiences openly.

I asked them to e-mail me their triumphs and tribulations so you can read them in their own words. You will also find excerpts from letters that readers of my other books and monthly E-Zine have sent me. At the end of the book there is a list of the first names of those who contributed. Some contributors requested anonymity – substitute names are marked with an asterisk.

If you take time to practise each SHYBUSTER, you'll soar away from shyness like a butterfly flees its caterpillar prison. I know, because I went from a hermit-teen who was terrified of people to a self-assured woman who now lectures around the country, does media interviews and feels comfortable at any gathering. If these SHYBUSTERs worked for a girl who was shy around her own shadow, they will definitely work for you!

" Shyness is a curse. Shyness makes me feel like I am an unwanted guest in everyone else's world. Shyness is the worst personality trait of all, without a doubt. I would rather be obnoxious and boorish than shy. Obnoxious and boorish people don't seem to be too bothered by being obnoxious and boorish at least. "

TONY V. – SYDNEY, AUSTRALIA

section I

a word to the shy...

don't be an avoidance junkie

Hooked on 'Hide and Seek'

Have you ever dodged anyone just to avoid making small-talk? All Shys have. If I saw an acquaintance coming towards me, I'd cross the street and pray he or she didn't see me. If there were a shop nearby, I'd dart into it until the coast was clear.

Some people say they've had an epiphany at the top of a Himalayan mountain or in a temple in India. Mine was walking along the street. I was window-shopping one Saturday morning when I was a nursery school teacher in Washington DC.

At one point I spotted a fellow teacher strolling towards me. Since I found Mr Fuller quite attractive, the thought of chatting with him was terrifying. In a panic, I dashed into the doorway of the shop I was passing.

I thought I was safe until I heard his voice behind me, 'Miss Lowndes, what are you doing here?' I was trapped like a fly under a glass. I pivoted slowly to venture a weak 'Hello' and, as I was turning, I saw what kind of shop I'd taken refuge in. It was a triple-X-rated boutique of 'adult toys'. When I finally mustered the courage to look at his face, Mr Fuller was sporting an enormous grin.

He winked at me and said, 'Was there anything in *particular* you were looking for, Miss Lowndes?' I bolted past him out the door, dashed down the street, and dove into a 'respectable' shop to sidestep him.

Needless to say, after that fiasco I never again made eye-contact with Mr Fuller. However, whenever we passed in the hall he'd say 'Good morning, Miss Lowndes' in a curiously salacious voice for a second-grade teacher.

Hearing his snide voice filled me with fury, not against Mr Fuller, but against my shyness. I declared war on it and was determined to win.

> **“ Whenever I avoided anyone on the street, it was a mental relief. I felt good because they didn't see me. I said to myself, 'OK, I won't do it next time.' But I always did. ”**
>
> AMANDA – LONDON, ENGLAND

Getting 'High' on Avoidance

When 'Socially Avoidant' people evade someone, it is more insidious than just a mental relief. It's not 'just mental', any more than taking heroin is just mental. It's physiological. You are actually getting a 'high' from the physical feeling, and it's harder to resist the next time.

For individuals with Socially Avoidant Personality, anxiety subsides following an avoidant response, thus reinforcing and escalating the avoidant response.[1]

3

SHYBUSTER 1:
Go Cold Turkey on the Small Stuff

Avoiding situations is an addictive drug. Right after, you get a mental high: *Whew, I escaped that one!* But it makes it all the harder because you crave that relief again and again. You dig a deeper rabbit hole that's harder to scurry out of each time. And, like an addict, you start to hate yourself for being so weak.

Start rehab now! Go cold turkey on dodging small encounters.

" Walking in the street and seeing someone approach from the front can be another terrifying experience. What helps is simply to greet the person in passing – a simple smile, nod of the head and a 'Hi' does wonders to break the awkwardness, and even builds a little confidence ('Wow, I said "Hi" and nothing bad happened, and he/she actually smiled back!')."

KOOS Z. – PRETORIA, SOUTH AFRICA

don't expect
a miracle
(today at least!)

TV Show: 'Fearful People Are Freaks'

Once while channel-surfing I got caught up in an ugly wave. I fell into one of those television talk shows, or rather circuses, where people who suffer from an assortment of afflictions are on display. This particular programme prefers people plagued with mental and/or physical disorders. The heartless host feigns compassion. He has an insatiable appetite for bizarre family relationships, strange sexual tastes and other eccentric infirmities. While tearful guests bare their souls to millions of viewers, the studio audience hoots and hollers, egging them on to even more humiliation.

'Ralph is afraid of peaches,' the host gleefully announces.

'Ooh,' the audience chants.

'He can't come near them.'

'Ooh,' the audience chants louder. Then, a basket of peaches appears on a big screen behind Ralph. The host points up at it. Ralph turns, swears (bleeped out), screams and jumps up. His 270 pounds of sheer terror races down the studio hall, followed, of course, by the camera crew.

Hysterical laughter from the audience.

Ralph, covered by three cameras, cowers in the corner backstage. At the host's goading, the audience begins chanting, 'Ralph come back. Ralph come back.' Ralph, still shaking, staggers back on the set.

The crowd applauds.

While winking at the audience the host asks Ralph, 'Why don't you like peaches?'

'They're fuzzy, they're slimy.' Then almost inaudibly, he mutters something about a girlfriend who had peach shampoo.

At that moment, two voluptuous women bring in two big baskets of peaches.

The audience's gleeful crescendo is 'Uh oh, he's in big trouble now.' At the sight of the peaches, the spectators are treated to a repeat performance from Ralph. This time he runs through the audience. They tackle him and succeed in pulling his pants down, which only adds to the ridiculousness of the spectacle. The camera catches the rear view of Ralph crawling away from the taunting audience, on all fours, his trousers around his knees.

Ralph once again crouches in the foetal position in a corner of the studio wings. The host follows and sneers, 'Do you know what you are now? A 6-foot tall, 270-pound man cowering in the corner?'

Mercifully for me, just then my phone rang.

Phobia Coach Cures Acrophobia to Zoophobia. Success Guaranteed. Walk-ins Welcome

When I came back 15 minutes later, Ralph was happily holding a ripe peach in his hands. With a big smile he brought it to his lips.

The camera cuts to a self-described 'phobia life coach' and 'therapist' sitting paternally beside Ralph. He explains to a gullible audience that he cured Ralph by gradual exposure and he will never fear peaches again.

The screen fades to black and advertises for a future guest: 'Do you have a child under the age of 13 who weighs over 300 pounds and is constantly teased and tormented?' Contact us at ...

welcome

Right Idea, Wrong Timing

Have you ever seen a nature film where a tiny flower bud grows taller in a few seconds? Two seconds later, it sprouts leaves. Another five seconds and exquisite petals open to receive the sunlight. The filming itself could have taken weeks. But we view the spectacle of nature in fewer than 30 seconds.

If Ralph's host were a horticulturist rather than an emcee of debauched demonstrations, he would try to convince us that the flower buds actually blossomed in seconds.

For Ralph, it was the right idea, but the wrong timing. Gradually exposing someone to a feared object or situation definitely works – but not in an hour-long show. Mental health professionals call it 'Graduated Exposure Therapy'. We'll call it 'GET' for short.

With successful exposure, social situations no longer cue danger-based interpretation and anxiety.[1]

Easy Does It

Dr Bernardo Carducci, a highly respected therapist who has researched shyness for 25 years, tells of a patient called

Margaret who was so petrified of spiders, she couldn't walk anywhere except on a wide pavement.[2] Her fear of spiders didn't permit her to enter any building but her own home.

The therapist treated Margaret with Graduated Exposure Therapy. First he asked Margaret simply to write the word 'spider' repeatedly. Her next task, probably weeks later, was to look at pictures of spiders in a book. It was a giant step, and probably a long time later, when she was able to view spider in a glass box across the room. Ever so gradually, Margaret could come closer to the little critter in the box.

As her final victory, Margaret sat comfortably in a room with a spider crawling along the arm of her chair.

But this was no hour-long TV show. By the end of the first hour, Margaret was still trying to hold her pen steady while she wrote the word 'spider.' Film coverage of Margaret's phobia and eventual cure would have made a rather humdrum TV show lasting probably several months. But at least it would be real.

Gradual exposure guides patients to confront feared situations and allows their fear to dissipate naturally. They interpret it accurately and gain essential skills. Patients gain a sense of safety through not prematurely escaping from, or avoiding social situations.[3]

Many Shys fail to shed their shyness because they think they have to force themselves to 'just do it.' They feel they need to accomplish the impossible, like winking at Mr Wonderful today or asking Ms Drop-Dead Gorgeous for a date tomorrow. Or swaggering into the boss' office and demanding a pay rise. Therapists would call this technique 'flooding'.[4] But who wants to drown? Just dip your big toe in first and go for the proven cure: Graduated Exposure Therapy.

> **❝ Do the thing you fear most and the death of fear is certain.❞**
>
> MARK TWAIN

SHYBUSTER 2:
Eat the Peaches at Your Own Pace

Your cure may be faster or slower than Margaret's. You won't have to sit down and write the word 'party' 100 times. Nor will I ask you to strut into a big bash tomorrow night. You will go at your own pace. But at least you know you're not swallowing snake-oil.

The Magic Combo to Kill Shyness

Some Shys think that gradually exposing themselves to scary situations isn't really the way to get over shyness. It's only natural to rationalize your way out of something you don't want to do. But it's an open and shut case. Hundreds, no, thousands of studies have proven it. The most effective way to get over being shy is to plan personalized exposure situations. *Always in the Kitchen at Parties* will help you do this. Using these exposure techniques while learning social skills is the magic combo for stamping out shyness.

Social Anxiety Disorder subjects receiving combination treatment of graduated exposure to fear-provoking situations and learning other-focused social skills improved significantly more on measures of community functioning and therapist ratings than did subjects with any other treatments.[2]

I'm sure many people have told you, 'You'll just grow out of it'. Are they right? Think about it this way. Simply by living on this earth, you are exposed to more and more situations as the years go by. And, naturally, you pick up social skills along the way. So, in a way they are right.

But who wants to wait years to shed their shyness? Jump in now. With the help of *Always in the Kitchen at Parties,* you can start your graduated exposure process immediately. You'll knock years off your suffering.

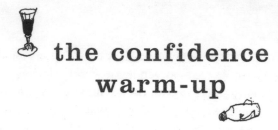

the confidence warm-up

The Energy Crisis

Researchers at the American Sociological Association scratched their scholarly heads and posed themselves a question: 'What type of personality are people most drawn to?'

They got on the case and quickly found the answer: *Someone who is energetic and optimistic.* Unfortunately these are not the qualities which immediately come to mind when you think of a Shy. In fact, one of the major obvious differences between a Shy and a Sure is energy level.[1]

Here is a way to rev up your engine so no one would ever suspect you're a Shy.

First, Become Unglued

Can you imagine a premiership footballer running onto the pitch without warming up? He'd get slaughtered in the first 10 minutes. Without warming up, a ballerina would hobble home on a toe splint. And a singer, without warming up, would bust a vocal cord. Why should a Shy try to be any different? You need to warm up for confidence.

Let's take an average day: You wake up. You clean your teeth. You shower. You get dressed. You eat breakfast. You walk out the door. Now a neighbour spots you. You utter a soft 'Hello' and quickly avert your eyes.

'Hmm,' she thinks, 'If she looks like a Shy, sounds like a Shy and acts like a Shy, she must be shy.'

Now let's change that scenario: You wake up. You clean your teeth. You shower. But this time you only don your pants. Now you look furtively round your bedroom and lock the door. You close the window and draw the curtains so the neighbours can't hear or see you.

Of course, you've already taken precautions. If you live with people, perhaps your spouse, your flat-mate or kids, you've explained your bizarre behaviour. And don't forget to familiarize the dog with this daily ritual so it doesn't attack. Now ...

SHYBUSTER 3:
Wake Up Like a Whacko

Run around the room in your underwear and flap your arms like a demented duck.

Shout like a crazed football fan.

Jump up and down like a rabbit on speed.

Laugh like a lunatic.

Whirl around like a tornado.

Fall back on the bed, kick your legs high in the air and shout at the top of your lungs 'Hoo ha, Hoo ha, Hoo ha. I'm making a fool of myself. And nobody cares!'

Ahem. Now stand up. Regain your poise. Smooth down your rumpled pants. Finish dressing. Comb your hair. Have a bite of breakfast. Kiss your spouse, kids or the dog goodbye. Now go out the door and greet the world with energy.

Oh, there's that nosy neighbour. Since your body, face and voice are warmed up and full of energy, it now feels natural to wave, smile and give a hearty 'Hello there.'

'Hmm,' she thinks, 'If she looks like a Sure, sounds like a Sure, and acts like a Sure, she must be sure of herself.'

You think I'm kidding about this exercise? Absolutely not! Exploding your energy sky-high in the morning, then letting it settle slightly, works a lot better than trying to haul it up out of a hole.

Naked Dancing

When you get really good at the above, start your day by dancing naked in front of the mirror. *Then* try to act shy!

section II

why am I shy?

take the 'cot test' to see if you were born shy

When the Doctor Spanked You Did You Take It Personally?

Before continuing, you should know the origins of your individual case of shyness so you'll know the best way to overcome it.

Are Shys born shy? Yes, some are. Some 20 to 30 per cent of babies are born with a brain chemistry which makes them more apt to become shy.[1] But genes are not your destiny. Nor is there a 'shy gene'. Scientists haven't looked into a microscope and said, 'Ah ha, there's the little blighter, the shy gene.'

If you were a sensitive baby (more prone to shyness), it will have shown up early. While you were busy discovering your toes and howling for your bottle, Mum and Dad could have figured out if you were the type of newborn that the shyness bug likes to feast on. Soon after they'd carried their little bundle of joy (that's you) home, you could have had the 'cot test' which replicates that of Philip Zimbardo, the Stanford professor who is considered by many to be the world's leading shyness researcher.

Here is all Mum and Dad would have needed. One: A weird toy – maybe a creepy black rubber spider. Two: Something stinky (no, not your own full nappy. That was an everyday fragrance for you). Three: the postman, a next door neighbour, or anyone else you had never met.

First step: Dangle the hideous toy above you. *Watch your reaction.*

Second Step: Wave the stinky stuff under your tiny nose. *Watch your reaction.*

Third step: Tell the stranger to say 'Koochie koo.' *Watch your reaction.*

Zimbardo and Jerome Kagan, a Harvard professor and leading shyness researcher, brought 400 one-month-old infants into their laboratory.[2] They put a creepy toy in the infant's cots, gave each a whiff of alcohol, and played a recording of a stranger's voice for them.

Almost a third of the babies freaked out, howling and flailing their tiny arms and legs. After their traumatic incident, they clung to a parent tightly. These are the babies who could become 'Highly Sensitive Shys' or 'HSS'.

In contrast, approximately two-thirds of the infants took it in their stride. They simply shoved the ghastly toy and stinky stuff away and smiled at the sound of the stranger's voice.

The researchers' hypothesis was proven:

Approximately one-third of babies' body chemistry makes them extra sensitive to unfamiliar events and people, and therefore more susceptible to becoming shy. [3]

66 As a baby, our daughter was so sensitive she couldn't stand being held by anybody but Mommy or Daddy (and sometimes even Daddy was not on her accepted list). It was a very trying time. She may have been colicky to start with, but as she grew older this sensitivity grew into what many might call 'shy', characterized by avoiding people's eyes when she first met them, not talking to them and hanging behind Mom and Dad's legs rather than socializing with people. 99

STEVE – VANCOUVER, BC[4]

Four Years Later

For Zimbardo and Kagan, however, the experiment was far from over. Four years after the first observation, they brought their 400 little subjects back into the lab. Sure enough, most of the tots who had tested as highly sensitive showed incipient signs of shyness.

The relentless researchers continued tracking the tykes' progress and determined that about half of those highly sensitive babies grew into being timid teens.

Parents, if your child seems extra-sensitive, start using SHYBUSTER 8 *Don't Baby Your Baby (page 35) immediately to curtail his or her possible shyness.*

SHYBUSTER 4:

Ask Them if You Freaked Out

If your parents are still alive, ask them about your 'cot behaviour'. Were you timid about your new environment? Or were you one of the calmer, 'Sure it's stinky and disgusting, but it's no big deal' babies?

Having been a highly sensitive baby does NOT mean you can't cure your shyness. But knowing what type of Shy you are helps you select a slightly different path and more realistic goal.

Today you essentially have the same nature you did when you were the little cot-crawler. Highly sensitive babies were overwhelmed by their little environment. Likewise, some highly sensitive adults are also overwhelmed by theirs – crowds, noises, bright lights.

“ My daughter is what her psychologist calls 'slow-to-warm'. She comes off shy until she knows someone, but eventually settles in and opens up, so people think she is just shy. It actually runs much deeper. It has to do with everything in her life. If she isn't

familiar with a situation, she has a significant amount of anxiety, even over the littlest of things. For example, she's in year 4 grade and her class was taking a trip to our state capital. She's been in this school with these kids since she was five, and has even shown her horse in Lansing a number of times, but she had never been to the state capital and didn't know what to expect. The night before the trip, she couldn't sleep, was nauseous, etc."

STEVE – VANCOUVER, BC

Many of us listen to outrageous radio and television personalities. We elect outgoing politicians, we listen to extreme rock bands, adore scantily-clad sexy show-off girls. We flock in droves to the cinema to see bigger-than-life movie stars – and then stay up half the night to see them again on the Oscars.

The highly sensitive person can feel like something's wrong with them because they're not a 'look at me' type. If you are a HSS, your brain functions differently from an extrovert's. It takes you longer to process information. You think more deeply. You try to listen carefully and usually speak more slowly. A number of Highly Sensitive Shys prefer country living rather than a big city of racing ambulances and deafening discos.

Does Being an Introvert Mean Being Shy?

Definitely not. Unfortunately, however, our Western world does not recognize or reward introvert qualities as much it does extrovert. Because this can make introverts question themselves, there is a high crossover between introverts and Shys.

Unfortunately, Shys often think they are not as smart or talented as the Sures. Stop! Wrong way! Go back! Countless studies have blasted the myth about shyness indicating stupidity. In many cases, it's just the opposite.

The majority of gifted children (60%) are introverts. In studies of intelligence, the higher the IQ, the higher the percentage number of introverts. A greater number of National Merit Scholars are introverted and they get higher grades in Ivy League colleges. [5]

What this says to a HSS is: Value your God-given qualities and don't let anyone make you feel inferior because you don't like to sit around with the gang and chew the fat, or leap into conversations before you've thought things through. Even extremely confident highly sensitive people need a little longer to process their thoughts. So give deserved worth to your inner world, and become comfortable with your quieter qualities.

Wanted: Thinker, Artist, Philosopher – Must Be Shy

HSSs usually are people of high integrity and compassion. They are not usually conspicuous leaders of crowds, but they are leaders by example: thinkers; advisors; healers. They are very fair and have many other qualities that make a positive impact on society.[6]

Recently, an extremely successful yet soft spoken woman named Cheryl engaged me to do a speech in Phoenix, Arizona. While driving to the convention hall, I told her I was writing a book on shyness. A few weeks later, she sent me this e-mail:

> " Leil, our conversation struck a familiar chord with me. I have struggled with 'shyness' all of my life, feeling like I'm marching to a different drummer than most of the world. I couldn't understand why many of my schoolmates and co-workers enjoyed talking with lots of people and spending large amounts of time visiting. I preferred just one or two close friends, more intimate settings, and deeper conversation. I couldn't figure out why I would rather remain in the background and think about a topic before speaking, while others would vocalize their thoughts without restraint. I couldn't fathom how people who became my closest and dearest friends would later tell me that they

thought I was 'cold' or 'aloof' upon first impression – but realized I was 'anything but' after they got to know me. I was very intelligent, always an honours student, and later an excellent businessperson. I truly liked people. But I couldn't seem to get the hang of the whole socializing bit. I wondered if something was 'wrong' with me.**"**

CHERYL – PHOENIX, ARIZONA

Cheryl's message continues with her self-discovery, her conclusions, and how she has come to lead a successful and joyful life within the framework of her more sensitive nature. It is very poignant but, due to its length, you will find the continuation of Cheryl's letter in the notes (see page 255).

did I 'catch' a dose of shyness?

Shake Your Family Tree for Signs of Shyness

Can you inherit shyness? Again, the reliable and revered researchers have ascertained the precise and unassailable answer to this question: 'Some do. Some don't.'

I don't mean to be sarcastic. Like inheriting long legs or brown eyes, it's a role of the dice whether you inherit shyness or not. However, a study called *Childhood Shyness and Maternal Social Phobia* found that children who had shy mothers are eight times more likely to be shy themselves. Twenty per cent of Shys have first-degree relatives with a phobia.[1]

SHYBUSTER 5:
Rummage Through Your Relatives

Having a shy relative is another possible ingredient in your particular shyness recipe. If you are interested in doing some detective work, ask your whole family – even your third cousin twice removed – if he or she had a great-aunt or -uncle whose parents were shy. Every relative counts!

If you've dug through your genealogy with a fine-tooth hacksaw and there are no suspects, there is yet another possibility.

Is Shyness a Communicable Disease?

You can't 'catch' a case of shyness. However, if your guardians, even if they weren't your parents, were shy, there is a greater chance you will be too, because we tend to imitate the people we are around, especially parental types!

> **“ My wife and I adopted a son who seems to have a very outgoing personality. I am scared to death that unless I change the way I am, he will lose that part of him. I would love to be an outgoing role model for him.”**
> SHELLEY – NEWCASTLE, ENGLAND

A child hardly ever recognizes that a parent is shy.[2] It's only these many years later that I realize that my mother was. One Thanksgiving when I was about 14, we were visiting a slew of relatives we hadn't seen in a long time. Aunt Lucy was jabbering away. Uncle Charley had a turkey hat on his head (and, I now suspect, a few drinks under his belt). My other relatives were chattering simultaneously. And there was Mama, sitting as quiet as a clam, hands folded. And I, like a little clamlet, sat silently beside her.

Parents, you are a role model for your kids. If you are shy, make an extra effort to whoop it up in front of your progeny. They will enjoy seeing you have fun and will follow your lead.

> **"** I never had any friends because we lived out in the country on a farm and there weren't many other kids who were my age around. The mothers of the other kids arranged a lot of times when they all got together to play. But my mother never did. When I got older, my Dad told me she was shy. Looking back, I wonder if the reasons I didn't have many friends is because she was too shy, and wonder if that's the reason she didn't call the other parents. **"**
>
> DINA – LANCASTER, PENNSYLVANIA

SHYBUSTER 6:
Did Shyness Rub Off On You?

If you're being a shyness-sleuth, look for clues that your parents or guardians were shy. You could even ask some of their friends.

was it bullies in bygone days?

Those Nasty Kids in the Neighbourhood

No worries about money. No worries about the job. No worries about love or sex. Wouldn't it be great to be a kid again?

Definitely not. Being a shy kid is worse than an adult who has no job, no money, and... Well, no job and no money.

Let's say you have conducted your research and find you are not a HSS. In fact your relatives say you were a confident little hellraiser as a toddler and young child. You would have grabbed that ghastly rubber spider and hurled it back at them. And say you've also shaken your family tree and found no shy suspects among your ancestors.

Is there another way the shy bug can find and gnaw away at you? Yes. I know because it took a big bite out of me.

A Raspberry to Remember

Time: Third grade
Place: Maths lesson
Cast: My classmates and me

The most difficult part of my school day was maths. Not because the numbers were mind-boggling. Not because I hated my teacher. But because of my acute shy-attacks. The teacher often gave us an exercise and then left the room for a few minutes. With furrowed brows, the girls would finish the exercise. Then they would start clucking like a bunch of baby chickens until the teacher returned. But I, the shy ostrich, buried my head in my books and pretended to be still working.

One unforgettable day the teacher gave us an exercise and then, as usual, left the room. During those silent working minutes, I felt the urgent need to pass wind (commonly known then as 'giving a raspberry'). I felt the wind flooding through me and I knew I would be unable to halt its escape. Thanks to our Maker, I managed to let the air out silently and slowly. It sailed away and, with a sigh of relief, I went back to tackling my assignment.

Fewer than 30 seconds later, one of the girls, Sonia, imitated a Japanese voice: 'Ah zoh,' she said, 'I smell raspberries.' Laughter from all.

'I wonder where it's coming from?' another girl chirped. More uproarious laughter.

'Let's find out!' Sonia pronounced. Then the nightmare began. Like an Easter egg hunt, Sonia began the festive search for the source of the scent.

Starting at the other side of the room, she crawled up and down each row dramatically sniffing everybody – much to the hilarity of all the confident girls who knew they were not culpable.

When she got to my row, I got hysterical. I grabbed my books and bolted out, tears streaming down my face. Racing down the hall, I heard a cruel chorus behind me chanting 'It was Leilie. It was Leilie. It was Leilie.'

Looking back, that was the pivotal point when my shyness went from bad to excruciating.

Fifty eight per cent of Shys can recall a traumatic social experience near the onset of their symptoms.[1] Forty four percent remember one intense episode, which they felt started it.[2]

Most little kids really don't mean to be cruel but, without thinking, they can be vicious. *The Journal of Clinical Psychology* cites a study called 'Peer Rejection in Early Elementary Grades' confirming the harmful effects of these early episodes.[3]

One single experience doesn't make a kid shy if he or she is not sensitive to start with. But it sure doesn't help! Even if Shys don't have one early horror story that they can point to, how well they feel accepted in school is crucial.[4] It becomes a template for their expectations in later years.

SHYBUSTER 7:
Replay the Early Show

Thoughtless youngsters can really mess up a sensitive little kid's head. If you're one of the 58 per cent of Shys who can remember one specific childhood experience, run it through your mind. Inevitably you will come to the conclusion that it was the other kids' cruelty, not your conduct that was at fault.

Contemplate it until you are convinced. It helps clear the path to confidence.

" Before I started school, therefore before I was even five years old, I had to go to hospital for what probably was only three or four days, but my memory is that it was an eternity. I was in a children's ward. I had the bed in the corner. I was the only boy in the ward and all the others were girls. But I would have been too young to understand gender difference. I would not talk to anyone. Some of the other children were quite loud and extroverted, they clowned around a lot. Particularly the girl in the bed in the opposite corner. I often cried. She would be the one to notice, and loudly make fun of it to all the others. I would roll over face-down and pretend to be asleep.

I was too shy to ask where the toilets were, so at least daily I would wet the bed. The nurses got increasingly angry that I kept doing this and yelled at me in front of the girls. "

NATHAN – GREEN BAY, WISCONSIN

it was all mum
and dad's fault

Dahling, My Shrink Said ...

Forty years ago in America, it was chic to have a psychiatrist. Anybody who was anybody (or who thought they were) decorated their conversation with, 'Well my shrink said ...'

Often the end of their sentence was, 'It was all my parents' fault.'

Whether psychologists actually did accuse parents or not, it was the common cop-out for any shortcomings. People paid dearly for this excuse.

To the point: Was it your parents' 'fault' that you became shy? Again, the revered and reliable researchers who have dedicated their lives to exploring the roots and results of shyness have come up with the answer: 'For some it was, for some it wasn't.' Overprotected children do, however, run a higher risk.

A study called 'Development of Anxiety: the Role of Control in the Early Environment' found ...

Parents who exert maximal control over a child's activities and decisions can negatively influence the child's sense of being able to control his or her own environment.[1]

I wish two of my long-time friends had known this. Steve and Lydia are a wonderful couple who have only one son. After he was born, Lydia wasn't able to have any more children, so little Lenny became obsessively precious to them.

If three-month-old Lenny started crying while I was visiting, Lydia would hop to her feet and sprint to the nursery. Sounds of her baby-talk would waft into the living room: 'Ooh, that's my iddy biddy baby. What was my widdle Lenny crying about? Did some big black bear come to bite my widdle baby? Awww, Mommy's here now. Everything is going to be all wight.'

Frankly, I found it disgusting. That doesn't mean if I had a kid, I'd lock him in the nursery and let him scream like a sick coyote. But I certainly wouldn't come running every time he hiccoughed.

When Lenny got old enough, Steve, Lydia and I would occasionally go to a restaurant. Sure enough, little Lenny would be in tow. Except Lenny wasn't so 'widdle' anymore. He was eight years old and, since he was the centre of their attention, adult conversation was futile. Whenever the little prince burped, there was a duet of 'Oh, Lenny. Are you OK?' 'Did the nasty Coca Cola make you burp?'

One evening, panicking because little Lenny burped three times in a row, Lydia said to Steve, 'Let's order him some orange juice.'

Upon hearing this, Lenny crossed his arms and announced 'I hate orange juice.'

'Well, darling, you drank it at Aunt Susan's last week,' Lydia said.

Louder than before, 'I hate orange juice.'

I was about to gag. I decided that, as much as I liked

Steve and Lydia, that was my last dinner with them unless they left their 'little darling' at home.

'Don't you think Lenny would enjoy eating at home next time?' I asked. 'I know a wonderful babysitter who cooks, too. My treat.'

'I hate baby sitters!' shouted the little brat. (Can you sense I was getting a tad emotional about this?)

Lydia leaned over and whispered, 'Lenny doesn't like baby-sitters.'

'I sort of picked that up,' I said.

'What other drinks can I have?' Lenny interrupted.

This was war. I looked right at Lenny and said, 'Lenny, why don't *you* ask the waitress?'

Lydia and Steve just laughed and called the waitress over. Lenny looked at his mother and loudly declared, 'I want a root beer.' Lydia then turned to the waitress. 'He'd like a root beer.'

'The waitress isn't hard of hearing,' I mumbled.

Where's Lenny Now?

We saw each other a few times more in the following year and, of course, the little prince always presided. The following summer my friends moved to Virginia because, they told me, 'Lenny would be in a better school system.'

I didn't see Steve and Lydia for 10 years, but recently I was giving a speech in nearby Washington, DC and called them. We decided on a restaurant and, for the first time, no Lenny!

When I asked after him Steve and Lydia looked at each other painfully. Lydia said, 'He didn't want to come.'

Hallelujah!

'Oh, that's too bad,' I said.

Steve and Lydia spent the next hour lamenting that the reason was he was 'uncomfortable around people'. He had no friends. He wouldn't go to parties. At 18, he'd never had a date. He was shy and felt the other kids didn't like him. 'So we home schooled him.'

I had to bite my tongue. It was obvious. By doing everything for Lenny and indulging his every whim, they'd kept him from ever developing the social skills or the courage to do things on his own.

Tell Your Kids to Go Play in Traffic

A slight exaggeration, of course. However, parents, do give your kids progressively more complicated challenges. Say you and your six-year-old are at a restaurant. And little Billy is served a jacket potato with butter and cheese on it. But, alas, little Billy doesn't like butter on his potato. He wants a new potato with just cheese.

'Mummy, I want just cheese. Tell her to take it back.'

Mum, your ideal response would be, 'Billy, why don't you tell her yourself? I'll call her over for you, but you must tell her.' Little by little, give your kids increasingly bigger challenges.

Mums, Don't Kiss It Better

Dads, congratulations. You are actually a better influence on your kids' shyness than your wife. Why? Because if another kid bullies your son and he comes home with a scratched knee, you are more apt to say, 'Get out there and tell him he can't treat you like that.'

Mothers, on the other hand, have been heard to say, 'Aww, honey. Let me kiss it better.'

In one study, fathers were so brusque about pushing their kids to stick up for themselves that even the researchers were shocked. But they had to admit it worked.

By pushing the child to change, thus appearing insensitive and intrusive, fathers may have influenced their sons to become less inhibited.[2]

This definitely does *not* mean to ignore them. Parents who have a strong bond with their children (love, open communication, dependability) and low control (encouraging them to do things on their own) are the most likely to have confident children.

SHYBUSTER 8:
Don't Baby Your Baby

Mums and Dads, this one's for you. I know it's because you love them, but do NOT do everything for your kids. Love them lots. Encourage open communication. Let them know they can depend on you. But progressively encourage them to do more and more on their own.

" My mother and I were very close, maybe because my father died when I was two and I am an only child. I don't know when it began, but I know by the time I got to primary school I realized that my mother was much more protective of me than the other kids' mothers. I wasn't even allowed to cross the street alone to play with the other kids. It didn't bother me that much because she would take me to the movies a lot and we'd go away together on every holiday. I liked that because I didn't have to be around other kids who would tease me. I think they thought I was a snob because I didn't play with them.

I was so shy in secondary school, especially around boys, that my mother put me in a small private tutoring school where we had only five or six people to a class. I'm 34 now and still live with my mother. I've hardly ever dated because I get so nervous around men that, the few times I have been asked out, I've said no. I realize I have to change but it's hard to break old patterns and thought habits. "

SHANNON – LIMERICK, IRELAND

so who ya gonna blame?

Most of us don't blame anybody. We're too busy trying to get over shyness. But there are some Shys who get angry and blame others for their condition. For them, I quote a great actress and, I've now discovered, a great philosopher, who fought a lifelong battle with shyness:

> **We are taught you must blame your father, your sisters, your brothers, the school, the teachers – you can blame anyone, but never blame yourself. It's never your fault. But it's always your fault, because if you want to change, you're the one who has got to change. It's as simple as that, isn't it?**
> KATHARINE HEPBURN

Yes, Katharine, it *is* as simple as that. But getting over shyness isn't. You can't just snap your fingers and instantly sound smart, suave, scintillating and not shy. It's like learning to ski. You need to practise each move before you can make all the right ones without having to give them a second thought.

section III

**dealing with people
until your shyness
is gone**

should I tell
people I'm shy?

Using the 'S' Word

It happens to all of us. Some well-meaning friend or family member blithely suggests, 'Well, why don't you just tell people you're shy? Then you'll feel more comfortable with them.'

So you consider it. You run and run a couple of scenarios through your mind:

If I tell them, what do I expect them to say? 'Oh you poor dear, you're shy? I understand what an awful feeling that must be. Well, I certainly want to become your friend and help you to get over it.'

Don't think so.

If I share my secret with a potential romantic partner, will he or she say, 'Oh, that's wonderful. I find shy people sooo sexy. Let's go out on a date and you can tell me all about it.'

Not likely.

So, for the moment, you decide not to tell.

Wise choice! I know from experience you will hear, 'Oh, not you! You've got to be kidding. You're not shy. I mean you're so nice, so friendly,' yada yada yada.

Let me interject an important note here. If, by chance, you are working with a therapist who encourages you to reveal your shyness, follow that counsel. Whatever your counsellor advises overrides any suggestion in this book. Each Shy is different and treatments vary.

" I am teaching my way through graduate school. And on the surface I guess I don't seem shy but my timidity is so painful that in order to not have to speak to familiar faces I will walk around, act occupied or just sit and listen (never putting in my opinion) to a conversation. Sometimes I tell people I'm shy and they just laugh. They don't believe me. They don't know how much I'm suffering inside."

ANGELA – HOPE, ARKANSAS

In high school, my mother was anxious about my sagging self-esteem and lack of friends. One Sunday evening after dinner, Mama suggested we talk about my shyness.

'Some other time, Mama.'

'Now!' Mama suggested I tell the girls I was shy.

'What, tell them?' That was like telling a boxer to lean right into the punch. The funny thing is, in a boxing match that works. But telling people I was shy would have had me down for the count.

'Promise me you will Leilie?'

'Mama, I can't.' She looked disappointed. 'I promise, Mama.'

That night I lay awake mopping tears out of my ears, and planning when to divulge my disgraceful secret. That time came much too soon. PE was just before lunch. Now or never. I entered the changing rooms early on what I now think of as D-Day (for 'Divulge Day'). Miss Popularity herself was already there. While getting into our shorts and T-shirts, Penelope started playing her favourite sport, small-talk, my weakest game.

The 'Big Confession'

'Well, Leilie, did you enjoy the weekend?'

My mind went into immediate selfconscious overdrive. *Should I tell her the truth, that I just hung around the house all by myself? Or should I fake an upbeat, 'Oh I had a fabulous time.' No, that's not a good strategy because she might counter with asking me what I did.*

By now the unspoken time-limit for a response, any response, was up. I returned her serve with an unskilled, 'Uh, yeah.'

Sure enough, then came the grand slam. 'What did you do?' Now I faced sure defeat. It was a choice of fibbing or 'fessing up' as Mama said. Courageously, I chose the later.

I looked down at my feet and blurted out, 'I'm shy.' Penelope seemed surprised and volleyed back the expected: 'What? Not you. You're not shy. You're kidding! I mean, you have no trouble talking to me ... Uh, well, see you later,' she said, scurrying off to class.

I wondered if I'd done the right thing.

I got my answer 24 hours later almost to the minute. The girls were opening their lockers and chatting like magpies when I arrived. 'Hi Leilie,' one shouted across the locker room. 'I hear you're shy. Is that true?'

Her comment was a cannonball in my stomach. As I was reeling from that one, another blasted me, 'What have you got to be shy about?'

Babbling about being nauseous, I dashed out of the locker room, up the stairs, and into an empty classroom. I missed lunch that day but I didn't care. I couldn't have eaten it anyway.

In retrospect, I realize that the locker room gang didn't intend to be cruel. In fact, they were probably trying to make me feel at ease. But like most people they were unskilled at dealing with someone shy. Besides, strangers and slight acquaintances don't care that you're shy.

SHYBUSTER 9:
Why Tell Strangers?

Unless you've been advised otherwise by a responsible mental health professional, there is no advantage to telling people that you're shy. Save the revelation for people who are important to you, your parents or close pals. (There are a few exceptions and we'll explore those later.)

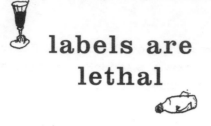

labels are lethal

You wouldn't hang a heavy sign round your neck with 'I Am Shy' scrawled on it. Revealing it to too many people, however, can often be just as much of an albatross. Besides, labelling yourself 'shy' is inaccurate. You are a complex mixture of an immeasurable number of qualities. To choose just one puts unnecessary emphasis on it.

Calling yourself shy could be a perilous self-fulfilling prophesy. When you tell people you're shy, you are not just telling others. You are telling yourself as well. *And that's the person who really counts.*

" Our daughter was on track to becoming terminally shy. One day after someone called her 'shy' I had a 'Eureka!' moment. I wondered if part of the reason why shy children become shy is that grown-ups call them shy when they exhibit shy behaviour around them. We see this all the time – 'Oh, aren't you the shy one?' or 'She's so shy, isn't she?' right in front of them as if they weren't there. When powerful people like grown-ups label us as shy, maybe we end up believing them and begin to self-label ourselves, developing that tendency most of us have to be a little reticent in the outside world into a fully-fledged personality habit called shyness.

Right then and there I talked to my wife and suggested that we never use the 'S' word to describe our daughter again, either in front of her or to other people. I also asked all our family members and friends not to describe her as 'shy', even if it was true at that time. Hopefully, if we didn't put a name to it, the shyness phase would pass.

It has definitely helped. While she's not the most outgoing kid in year 7, she is perfectly happy telling kids and adults stories and jokes, and has developed a fundamental self-confidence that is definitely not shyness. Kids are listening all the time, aren't they, so we better be careful with what we say around them!"

STEVE – VANCOUVER, BC[1]

When a Label Stopped the Music for Me

I don't think I was destined to be a singing diva. However, someone slapped a label across my lips when I was in the seventh grade. Nary a note came out of my mouth again – at least not an on-key one.

In 7th grade I sang in the church choir. One afternoon during a rocky rehearsal, the choirmaster turned his stern face directly towards me. '*Someone* is off-key. I want that someone to just mouth the words.' There was no mistake who that off-key someone was. And from that day on, I sang like a crow with a cold. I still just mouth the words to 'Happy Birthday.'

A few years ago I was listening to the radio with an old classmate who knew I was severely musically challenged. They were playing the top 40 songs that were popular when I was in sixth grade. Just for fun I started warbling along with the radio. When I'd finished, my friend said,

'Leil, that's perfect!'

'Perfect what?'

'Perfect pitch.'

'Couldn't be.'

'Was!'

'Couldn't be!'

'Was.'

Tentatively I tried a few more songs from those years. We were both staggered because I was right on key. But, here's the mind-boggler: I could not sing even one song that came after that fateful 'Someone is off-key' day. The choir master *labelled* me tone deaf. Therefore I was tone deaf. A self-fulfilling prophesy.

SHYBUSTER 10:

Don't Burn Yourself with the 'Shy' Branding Iron

Do not succumb to that deadly virus called 'self-fulfilling prophecy'. Just like the American Association of People with Disabilities wisely says, 'Someone in a wheelchair is not "handicapped" or "disabled".' They are just like able-bodied people. They simply carry one more piece of baggage. And you simply carry a surplus bag called 'shyness'. Fortunately for you, you'll soon be able to leave that unwanted baggage behind.

tell the truth, the half-truth, and nothing but the half-truth

How to Get Out of a Situation You're Not Ready for – Yet!

Suppose a friend asks you to call 20 people and tell them of the upcoming World Cup Party. But you're still too shy to talk to 20 strangers. Is it better to 'confess' that you're shy? Or should you find another excuse for wriggling out of their request?

Actually, neither. Take the middle road and half-tell them by *alluding* to your shyness in a lighthearted fashion. This way you don't make them the least bit uncomfortable, yet they get the point.

Go ahead and use the 'S' word, but just in passing. Say something like, 'Well, a shy guy like me couldn't talk to 20 people in one day.' Or, 'If you were as shy as I am, you'd rather die than make 20 calls.'

Some Savvy Shys Prefer to Laugh and 'Warn' People

If this is your choice, do it in a manner that won't make either you or them uncomfortable. Say you're shy – but with a big smile and a 'So what's the big deal?' attitude. Divulge it with

---

SHYBUSTER 11:
I'm Shy, So What?

When you pass your shyness off casually, it slides off others like a satin sheet. Having told them in a lighthearted manner can come in very handy later when they ask you to make the calls. Laughingly remind them. 'C'mon, I told you I was shy,' is much better than 'I can't do that. I'm too shy.' But don't use this SHYBUSTER as a cop out!

---

lightheartedness like you're saying, 'I feel fantastic today.' People listen to your tone of voice and body language much more than your words. But you knew that already.

Is Shyness 'Charming'?

I should mention that there are many people who find shyness charming, and it is, in a way. Everyone would prefer a Shy to a boisterous egoist. Nevertheless, being considered 'charming' is not worth the pain that goes with it.

> " I have always been shy. I hardly talked around anyone except my family. Even though I was fairly pretty, I only had a few dates in high school and they were

disasters because I didn't know what to say. I'd usually pretend I had a headache and that that was the reason I didn't talk much. Then I'd be taken home and I'd cry.

Then I moved to Philadelphia, where I had only one boyfriend and he treated me more like a trophy than a person with ideas. We would go out to dinner with some of his friends and I think he liked that I was silent. He'd call me his 'little doll'. I'd act like I liked it but he didn't know how much I was suffering inside."

LAURA – PHILADELPHIA, PENNSYLVANIA

section IV

what people *really*
think of you

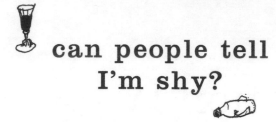

can people tell
I'm shy?

Everybody's Laughing at Me

You probably imagine a bumper sticker on your forehead warning everyone, 'I have Social Anxiety Disorder.' So they ridicule you or run.

Not true! Most people are oblivious to your shyness. Unfortunately, Shys think everybody is concentrating on them – when people are really preoccupied with themselves.

> **❝ My father helped cure me of my shyness by telling me, when I was about 14, that actually everyone is normally so busy thinking about themselves, and worried what you are thinking about them, that they are not focusing on you nearly as much as you think. I saw it immediately. It is so mind-blowingly obvious once you see it. ❞**
> **PENNANT – LONDON, ENGLAND**

When your heart sounds like a repeater pistol in your chest, it's hard to believe others can't hear it. Don't they see your face slowly beginning to resemble a sunburned lobster? But unless you are shaking like a chicken on a caffeine buzz, most people have no idea that you're shy. In fact, there is a good chance they are shy, too.

About 13 per cent of people in Western countries are lifetime Shys. Eighty per cent say that they have had a shy period in their lives. And 40 per cent say they are still anxious about themselves and the impression they're making.[1]

The Great Pretenders

My shyness seminars often took place in a hotel where other seminars were scheduled at the same time. Many times an extremely outgoing person would be in the queue to sign in for my seminar. He or she might be talking to others waiting, or joking with the registration person. In these cases I'd go over to these 'extroverts' and quietly ask if they were signing up for the right seminar. They'd give me a big smile and assure me they were.

At first I was confused but, as the seminar progressed, I discovered that many apparently confident people were excruciatingly shy – they just covered it well. No one would guess that these gregarious people suffered great inner turmoil.[2] Outwardly confident people can be secretly self-conscious and constantly putting themselves down. Even while they are laughing and chatting, they are painfully obsessed with what others think of them.

" My shyness isn't what I would call 'typical'. I am 32 years old and I come across as confident and friendly, the latter of which I am, not sure about the first. This is because, when I meet new people in a social gathering for instance, I'll confidently say 'Hallo,' but I tend to be self-conscious in ways that stifle my wish to strike up meaningful conversations. Strangers give me the creeps but yet, ask any of my friends and contemporaries, they'll say I am an up-front go-for-it sort of guy. I read somewhere that, scared or not, just pretend and no one will notice the difference. I am afraid that's me. I don't want to pretend to be confident when really I am mush-mellow beneath. It's just so much work mentally (and I hate sweaty palms!). "

PETER B. – PERTH, AUSTRALIA

Confidence-pretenders may look like they are enjoying themselves but their suffering can be even more excruciating than most Shys. People often expect them to help with a project or attend an event which, due to their shyness, they refuse. How many times can they come up with an excuse not to pitch in or party with friends? People may start to mistrust or dislike them.

People Are Way Off Base

Tons of recent research confirms that neither Shys nor non-Shys can spot shyness accurately. Randomly picking one study out of the sociological hat, researchers looked for a group of people who had a fairly close association with each other. They chose 48 students who lived in the same college dorm.[3] These students chatted with each other in the breakfast room and attended classes together. They saw each other around campus, studied together in the evenings, and even partied together on weekends. In other words, the inhabitants of this dorm knew each other *very* well.

First the researchers sequestered each individual student to gather confidential information on how shy she or he really was. Once they had this data, they asked all of the students to assess secretly each of their dorm-mates' degree of shyness.

The results astounded the researchers. They discovered that many of the shy students were judged 'not shy' by 85 per cent of their dorm mates. Conversely, some students who considered themselves to be exceptionally confident were dubbed 'shy' by some of their colleagues.

So if you're queasy about people detecting your shyness, relax. I promise you, it doesn't show anywhere as much as you think it does.

SHYBUSTER 12:
Be Shy on the Sly

You think your shyness sticks out like a wart on your nose? No way. Ninety per cent of the time nobody can tell. And if by chance they do pick up on it, they don't dislike you for it. They're in your court and only sorry that you're suffering from it. They too would like to see you emerge from your shell. Later we'll discuss when, how, and *if* it's better to tell people – and whom to tell once you decide.

" Nobody thought of me as shy. But my mind would be spinning like a gyro while I attempted to respond intelligently to the teacher's query. Following the inevitable failure would come the inevitable embarrassment. Then the standard sinking feeling, wanting to disappear into myself, into a crack in the wall, trying to become as small as possible, invisible if I could.

Even now, if someone asks me a question, my mind is racing in a hundred directions at once. My head is pounding out of my chest. I may look composed, while inside I am in tumultuous agony. "

BRUCE – BOULDER, COLORADO

take off your mud-coloured spectacles

Don't Nitpick for Negatives

You are talking with someone. You fear they think you're an idiot, that you brought your clothes at a jumble sale and combed your hair with an egg-beater this morning. Pitch the paranoia and realize that this is simply not true. You only imagine that people feel negatively towards you.[1]

How's this for an ingenious study? Several researchers hired actors, a cameraman, and bought some strange props. They then filmed the individual actors facing directly into the camera saying, 'Hello,' 'Hi,' etc. as though they were meeting someone for the first time.[2]

The researchers directed one-third of the performers to have a warm, accepting 'I like you' demeanour. One-third were to have a cool 'You bore me. In fact, I don't like you' look on their faces. They asked the rest to give the camera completely neutral expressions as they pretended to be meeting someone.

Of course the resourceful researchers didn't want to depend entirely on the acting acumen of the thespians in the film. To assure scientific accuracy, they put a fragrant scent like a bouquet of flowers under a third of the actor's noses to encourage a pleasant and accepting demeanour. The unfortunate second third were filmed with an unspeakably revolting glop under their noses. Nothing was put in the vicinity of the noses of the 'neutral-expression' actors.

I Just Know They Hate Me

When finished, they showed the film to a group of subjects, half of whom were confident and the other half shy. Both the Shys and the Sures were told to imagine the performers in the film were meeting them personally for the first time. Pen or pencil in hand, they had to gauge if each actor in the film liked them or not.

The results? The Shys felt most of the faces were snubbing them, or neutral at best. They even interpreted some of the warm expressions as social rejection. Whereas the dozen Sures felt most of the faces were positive towards them, or neutral at worst.

The 'jury' had reported. The verdict was in:

Shy individuals imagine signs of disapproval or rejection that do not come from external stimuli but from long-term memory and internal cues. As such the individual's evaluation is not objective. It is prone to negative distortion or bias.[3]

SHYBUSTER 13:

Pitch the Paranoia

Stop looking for rejection. It's your own imagination working overtime. Ninety-nine per cent of the time, you are wrong if you think someone is rejecting you.

He Said, She Said

Have you ever had a painful social experience and couldn't get it out of your mind? All Shys have. That's one of our specialities.

You go over and over what *they* said, what *you* said, then what *they* said again, then what *you* said ... ad nauseum. Every time you run the scenario through your mind, it's worse.

My best friend in boarding school was an expert at that. Stella looked like porcelain Barbie doll (this was pre-women's movement when being called a 'Barbie Doll' wasn't an insult). But in spite of her beauty she was incredibly shy, just like me. Shys stubbornly refuse to believe good things about themselves.[4]

Our girls' school had a monthly mixer with a nearby boys' school. Of course, Stella and I always hung around the sidelines trying look cool and disinterested. A lot of the girls were eyeing a 'dreamboat' (the archaic word we used then) named Shawn. Over the summer he had broken up with the most popular girl in our class – much to the glee of our school's entire female population.

At the first dance of the year, during our 'Ho hum, who cares about boys?' charade, Shawn smiled at Stella from across the room, then came over and mimicked a deep bow. 'May I have the pleasure of this dance Madam?'

Shawn must have noticed her reeling from the shock because he smiled, gently took her hand and guided her to the dance floor. I ducked behind a pillar to spy on them. From my strategic position, I saw my friend gradually becoming more relaxed with him.

At one point, Shawn noticed someone over her shoulder. Apologetically , Shawn excused himself. Stella's face dropped like a fallen soufflé. She quickly scurried over to me. 'Leil, we are getting out of here.'

'What?'

'Now! Right now!'

Life Is the Pits

All the way back to the dorm, Stella whined miserably. 'I just knew he'd be turned off. I was boring him. He was just being kind to someone who looked lonely.'

'Stella, you're nuts. There could have been any number of reasons Shawn left. Maybe he had to go to the bathroom and felt it was inappropriate to say that to a girl. Maybe he had to make a phone call. Maybe he ...'

Stella didn't hear me. 'He was just doing his good deed for the week, dancing with a dog to try to make her feel better. He probably already has a new girlfriend and didn't want her to see him dancing with anyone else.

Maybe he ...' to Stella, the whole encounter was a disaster.

Several weeks later, we were scarfing down a hot-fudge sundae at the counter of the local drugstore. Suddenly Stella turned as white as a turnip and swivelled her stool towards me so her back was to the door.

'Stella, what's the matter?'

'Shh. Keep your voice down. He just walked in.'

'He who?! What he?'

'*Him*, Shawn – the guy who stranded me on the dance floor.'

I looked over Stella's shoulder and, sure enough, it was Shawn, making a beeline straight towards Stella's back. As he came closer, he put his finger to his lips to signal me to 'Shh, don't tell Stella.'

Then Shawn gently tweaked her pony-tail. 'Hey, pretty girl, what happened to you at the party?'

Stella was speechless, so I filled in, 'Uh, shortly after you left, we had to, uh, be somewhere by, uh, 8.30.'

Shawn was surprised. 'I didn't leave. I spotted a buddy giving me the fish-eye because I owed him 10 bucks. So I went over to pay him back and restore his faith in humanity.'

He lowered his voice and smiled at Stella 'then I went to the buffet table to get us both a snack. When I came back, you were gone.' He put his hand on his heart and bent his head in mock despair.

I looked at my watch, 'Oh my goodness, look at the time,' I lied. 'I have to go now or I'll be late for my appointment.'

'Uh, what appointment?' Stella stuttered.

Dummy! 'Oh you know.' But, of course, neither of us did.

When I reached the sidewalk, I peeked through the

coffee shop window. I saw Shawn smilingly slide onto the stool I had just vacated.

Life Is Beautiful

A few hours later Stella sailed into our dorm room and started dancing. At that moment, she resembled a Barbie doll more than ever – pony-tail swinging, cheeks red, and a permanent smile plastered on her face. She told me Shawn had asked her out for the following Saturday night.

> **Individuals with high levels of social anxiety often experience numerous highly intrusive and interfering thoughts about past unsatisfactory social events, which lead them to recall the events as more negative than they were.**[5]

When you're nervous meeting new people, it's not just psychological. Biology gets into the act, too. Researchers have monitored both Shys' and Sures' brain activity while being introduced to strangers. They discovered that Shys had 'exaggerated activity in the amygdala and related medical temporal lobe' Huh? In normal English, this translates into: Shys suffer high *physical* anxiety.

Your amygdala really does a jig when you meet people who might be important to you – like job interviewers, bosses, potential friends, office superiors, and attractive people who are potential partners. The physical reaction can be so powerful that your mind goes blank and English becomes a second language.

For some people, this only happens in particular situations. They are 'selectively shy'.

> **“ Whenever I'm sitting at my desk and my supervisor comes over, my shyness problem jumps to the forefront once again. I am very comfortable and talk all the time with the people in my department. But I feel this woman is always judging me.”**
> DONNA – DUBUQUE, IOWA

One very prevalent and painful type of selective shyness is 'love-shy'. Even people who are not shy in most situations can fall prey to this. When they meet someone sexually attractive, they become unglued. Forget asking for a date, they can't ask an attractive person for the time of day without muttering like a drunken duck.

> **“ I'm fine with most people but when I see someone who looks exciting, my shyness is like a little devil sitting on my shoulder telling me not to go and talk to her, what if she has a boyfriend, what if she laughs at me, etc. The devil is still in control. I hate the thought of being alone for the rest of my life.”**
> TROY – VANCOUVER, CANADA

don't be a sucker for rejection

If You Accept Me, I Don't Accept You

Groucho Marx, taking a puff on his cigar, 'I would never join a club who would have me as a member.' Some Shys subconsciously agree with him. Especially younger Shys still in school, who may want to be part of a self-appointed 'elite' group of students. When they are not welcomed, they feel something is wrong with them. But even when they *are* welcomed, they still feel something has gone amiss somewhere.

People who blatantly reject you are not worthy of your admiration. Don't try to break into their circle. You're just setting yourself up for a confidence game where you'll lose. A study called 'Popularity, Friendship, and Emotional Adjustment' determined that disapproval, real or imagined, by anyone you admire colours your feelings towards yourself.[1] That imagined distorted colour of yourself lasts a very long time, long after you've forgotten the names of the disapprovers.

> ## SHYBUSTER 14:
> # Don't Choose Toxic Friends
>
> ---
>
> Choose your friends carefully. Just because someone
> is 'popular' it does not mean they are worthy of
> your esteem. Do not try to socialize with people
> who you know do not accept you. It sabotages your
> self-esteem.

Men are especially susceptible to the 'want the ones who
don't want you' syndrome. Mr Shy goes to a party and sets
his sights on the best-looking woman there. For half the
party he fantasizes about how he's going to make the
approach, Finally he gets up the courage.

'Hi!'

She turns the other way.

Crash! His self-esteem craters. Sad Mr Shy slinks back to
the bar feeling defeated and all the more shy.

Meanwhile there is a lovely lady across the room who
has been eyeing him all night. Think how terrific he'd feel
about himself if he'd talked to her and she'd shown her
interest.

Bill Gates was a reject from the cool crowd but he didn't
bemoan the fact that popular colleagues didn't accept him.
The boys who put the first computer together in a garage
weren't the 'in crowd.' So who's had the last laugh now?

**come back down
off the ceiling**

Shoot the 'My Life' Movie

If you were a film-maker and shot the same motion picture
twice with the same actors, costumes, set and script – but
from different angles – it would look like a different movie.
Likewise, the same real-life scene viewed by a Shy and by a
Sure have very different perspectives.

Let's say you are happily snuggled in your seat munching popcorn at the movies. You are captivated by the characters on the big screen. You pass judgement on which
ones you like and which ones you don't. You hope the
good guy gets the girl and the bad one gets the boot. You
even form opinions about the supporting characters – he's
a dupe, she's a doll, he's deep, she's shallow. You aren't
thinking about yourself. You don't stress over what they
think about you. You are observing *them*. You are comfortably inside your body looking out. Sociologists call this
the 'field perspective'.[1]

To a great extent, this is the way super-Sures see the
world. They reside securely in their own skins looking out at
the 'field'. They form impressions about others and don't
fret much about what other people think of them. Sures
simply *assume* they will be accepted. Not so, Shys. You automatically feel people will reject you and that you need to
prove yourself.

> People usually view situations from a 'field
> perspective'. Socially-phobic individuals view
> situations from an 'observer perspective'.[2]

Your Out-of-Body Experience

Many Shys, remembering an uncomfortable situation,
mentally float outside their bodies and see themselves as
they *suppose* others saw them. It's like they're drifting
around the room observing themselves, judging themselves,
criticizing themselves. It could be called an 'out-of-body
experience'. Mental health professionals prefer the designa-
tion 'observer perspective'.[3]

> Upon entering a social situation, socially phobic
> individuals form a mental representation
> of their external appearance and behaviour
> as an audience might see them.[4]

Think back to a recent experience where you felt comfortable – perhaps a summer picnic with your family. You all
were seated at a wooden table in the woods, happily
munching hot dogs and guzzling down coke. You watched
your little nephew as he dribbled mustard down his chin.
What a messy kid, you thought.

Your brother-in-law started sounding off on how hot
dogs are made. You mumbled to yourself, *He thinks he's the
expert on everything. Wish he'd shut up.* You smelled the
hot dogs on the grill behind you. *Umm, smells good, I'd like*

another. So, of course, you hop up and get one.

You are now in the 'field perspective'.[5] In other words, you are viewing the scene from your perspective. You form your own opinions.

You weren't thinking, *Everyone notices I haven't said a word. They probably think I'm dense. I'm hungry. Should I ask to have another hot dog, or should I just go get one? No, better not. They'll think I'm greedy. Besides I'd probably spill mustard on my shorts and they'll think I'm clumsy. I don't think anyone here likes me anyway.*

Afterwards, of course, you run that painful reel over and over in your head. You are wretched, slithering outside your body and seeing yourself from the outside.

SHYBUSTER 15:
Stamp Out the Surreal

The next time you think about a past social situation, do not float around the room criticizing yourself as an observer. Jump right into your body and form opinions on what *you* think of *them*. Force yourself into the 'field perspective'. Keep yourself out of the picture.

think of your shyness from their perspective

Shys Don't Play Stupid Games

Have you ever seen a play where the actor forgot his lines? How did you feel? Did you look down on him? Of course not. You were just uncomfortable for him.

That's the way some Sures feel around a Shy. They don't dislike you. They just feel *your* discomfort and don't know to handle it. Awkward or unsophisticated people can feel it 'cramps their style'.

Bantering and teasing are trademarks of the average Briton's personality, especially with younger or less cultured people. Highly sensitive people aren't used to putting other people down, even in fun.

Men especially like to joke around with each other. 'Hey Fatty, are you always this stupid or are you making a special effort today?' Or, 'Baldy, I know you love nature – in spite of what it did to you. Ha ha ha.' They dish out an insult to a buddy, expect him to chew it up and spit back a supposedly better witty putdown.

Can't Take It, Can Ya Buddy?

Teasing is not a pretty game, but it is fun for the insulters. It can be fun for the 'insultees' too, but *only* if they know how to sling the slurs back. A tennis pro doesn't enjoy playing with a newbie who has never hit a ball. And there's no thrill in razzing somebody who can't spar.

This foolish banter isn't just a guy thing. Women enjoy something similar. Rather than mocking each other, girls often giggle about an absent colleague. Frank Sinatra called it 'dishing the dirt with the girls'. They're not malicious. They're just upholding the teen stereotype.

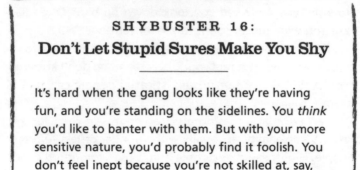

SHYBUSTER 16:

Don't Let Stupid Sures Make You Shy

It's hard when the gang looks like they're having fun, and you're standing on the sidelines. You *think* you'd like to banter with them. But with your more sensitive nature, you'd probably find it foolish. You don't feel inept because you're not skilled at, say, tiddlywinks. So why feel inadequate that you don't play an even more stupid game?

slay the
monster memories

It Wasn't as Bad as You Think It Was

The 'Putting Yourself Down' plot thickens. Not only do you fathom rejection when there is acceptance, you don't remember social situations accurately. Looking back you see monsters that were never there. (Please keep in mind that I'm using the word 'you' instead of 'most Shys' only for simplicity. You probably know what pertains to you and what doesn't.)

**Shy subjects recall a pleasant social situation
more *negatively* than it was.[1]**

It Starts Early

Even Shy toddlers have fuzzy negative recall of fun things. In a study called 'Individual Differences in Children's Eyewitness Recall: the Influence of Intelligence and Shyness', teachers rated kids on intelligence and, separately, on shyness.[2] Then they all went off to a birthday bash for one of their classmates. It was a real kid-pleaser: balloons, birthday cake, presents, singing happy birthday, the works.

A week later, researchers tested the kids to determine how much they remembered about the pleasant party.

They asked each one:

    'What did the cake look like?'

    'What games did you play?'

    'Did you have a good time?'

The researchers even threw in a few ringers like, 'What happened when the poor clown dropped the ball?' But there was no clown and no ball at the party.

Clean Your Binoculars

The results: Intelligence had very little to do with the accuracy of the kids' recollections. The deciding factor was how shy they were. The confident kids remembered the events far more enjoyably and accurately than the shy tykes. The Shy kids concentrated on negatives, especially those which involved themselves. It's as though the sure kid viewed the pleasant party through clear glass, and the Shys saw it through a dirty mirror. Their own pessimistic self-image blocked the view.

Shy adults do the same. The more you think back on an event, the worse it gets in your memory. The best way to remember something accurately is to write it down before your cynical imagination gets carried away.

SHYBUSTER 17:
Be Your Own Social Scribe

Right after a social situation, write your *immediate* impressions. If retroactively you remember anything negative about the encounter, go back and check your notes. If that embarrassing or disappointing moment isn't in your notes, *forget it*. It didn't happen.

Subjects with Social Anxiety Disorder often forget or distort pleasant experiences.[3]

Don't Watch the Re-runs

That study is called 'Post-event Processing in Social Anxiety' and my friend Stella certainly proved the point. She was an expert at negative 'post-event processing'.

She and I were eating lunch with a girlfriend a few weeks after she'd met Shawn. Since Megan hadn't seen Stella since she'd started dating him, she was dying of curiosity.

'How did you meet him Stella?' Megan panted.

'Um, at the September mixer,' Stella replied.

Megan wanted more. 'I mean how? Did he come over to you? Did you go over to him? I want the whole story.'

'I don't know. We just started talking.'

'Don't be so coy, dahling,' Megan teased.

'I don't remember!' Stella snapped.

'OK, OK Stella, don't take it personally.' Megan looked at me and shrugged. I too was surprised at Stella's irked response.

When we were back at the dorm I asked Stella, 'Why didn't you want to tell Megan how you and Shawn met?'

'Leil, I told the truth. I really don't remember the details.'

'Well, what *do* you remember?'

She thought for a minute. 'Well, I remember he left the dance before us.'

Now I was relentless. 'Why? Why do you think he left?'

'I dunno, I guess he was just bored and didn't want to dance with me any more.'

'Stella!' I shouted 'Don't you remember the buddy he owed 10 bucks to? Of course he liked you. He asked you out.'

Stella rolled her eyes. 'Yeah, but I don't know how long that will last.'

My friend was hopeless. Like a typical Shy, she didn't even remember the pleasant parts, only the painful. She'd re-run it in her mind so much that it became the only part she'd ever remember.

Individuals suffering from social Phobia remember negative experiences longer than positive experiences.[4]

Log It as a Cold Case

If you remember pleasant things about a past social situation, great. However, if bad memories start to flood over you, check your post-happening notes. Replaying a negative tape can be dangerous to your mental health – and fatal to your confidence.

> **❝ It's not that I don't like to be with new people. I tried and signed up for a hiking trip offered by the community centre. Everybody was talking as we were walking. I just hung back and sometimes I'd see one of them look back at me and fake a smile. Then they'd say something to the person walking with them. I know they were commenting to each other that I was stupid or something. ❞**
> **WELLINGTON – AUCKLAND, NEW ZEALAND**

Penny, no offence intended, but you probably remember it all wrong. Just like my dear dismal friend Stella who only remembered that 'Shawn deserted her on the dance floor.' Your hiking friends' smiles were probably sincere. It was a way to let you know you were welcome to catch up and talk with them.

Get Real

'Thanks a bunch, Leil,' you may be saying. 'You've just told me that I'm seeing social situations through a muddy lens. Then you say I remember it pessimistically and it gets worse each time I think of them! Then, to top it off, you're saying I'll only remember the negative parts. Thanks for the bad news.'

No, Shys, don't you see it's good news?! I have given you sociological proof that ...

1. Most people don't have any suspicion that you are shy.
2. Social situations aren't anywhere near as bad as you feel they are while you're in the middle of them.
3. Retrospectively, you were much better than you remember. Other people's negative reactions are largely a figment of your imagination.

Why is this good news? Because, although past incidents can't be changed, your interpretations – past, present, and future – can be.

'We've talked about the good news. So what's the bad news?' you ask. The bad news is you didn't know how good things were at the time. You could have enjoyed them a whole lot more if you had.

I think I'm beginning to love you, self

Getting to Know and Love Yourself

Sadly, even though Shys concentrate on themselves, few develop a solid sense of identity. Most really don't know themselves. And how can you love someone you don't know?

Many social phobics never feel complete. They never attain a satisfactory 'sense of self.'[1]

In the 1960s technology empowered us to travel to outer space. Now technology allows us travel in the other direction, inner space. Thanks to neuroimaging, hardly a week goes by when scientists don't discover unknown regions of the brain which hold mysterious memories and incredible emotional experiences.

You probably don't want to shave your head, go to a lab and wire your brain for magnetic resonance imaging to see why you act the way you do. But you can do the next best thing. A potent weapon to battle shyness is called self-knowledge. It is not a long or strenuous trip. It is surprisingly easy for the value you receive.

Invest Just Five Minutes a Day for a Priceless Gift

Self-knowledge is knowing how you, personally, feel about a wide range of issues – especially profound questions. Here is how to achieve that knowledge which adds a confident wisdom to your personality.

Choose a quiet time each day – perhaps while shaving, putting on makeup or travelling to work. Or maybe just before going to bed. Interrogate yourself as though you were a radio host interviewing yourself, and answer one soul-searching question each day. Ponder it thoroughly. Even if you have a quick answer, continue focusing on that concept for the full five minutes so it is deeply embedded in your psyche. You'll never again be intimidated or at a loss for words when deep subjects come up.

Some sample questions could be:

Do I have a purpose on earth? If so, what is it?
Who is the God of my understanding?
What do honour, success, family, friendship mean to me?

You'll find 116 more self-knowledge questions on page 259. They comprise your first months of self-exploration.

Your self-interview might go something like this:

'Self, if you had a lot of money to donate to a charity, which one would it be?'

Well, you know Self, I've never really thought about it. But every time I see a blind person, my heart goes out to them. I always wish I could give them their sight back, but of course that's not within my power. I guess I'd donate to help research on blindness.

'That's wonderful, Self.'
Well, thanks, Self, but, hey, that's just me.

SHYBUSTER 18:

Find Your Passion and Your Purpose

You will be thrilled with how quickly you cultivate a significant sense of who you are. As you listen to your own answers, you'll also see you are a pretty admirable person, and there is no need to be shy.

In addition to giving yourself one of the greatest gifts of a lifetime, you will never hesitate when meaningful subjects come up in conversation. You won't need the extra time to formulate your ideas. You've already done that.

The self-knowledge questions at the back of the book are just for starters. When you finish them, write and answer more of your own devising.

section V

getting out of
the kitchen

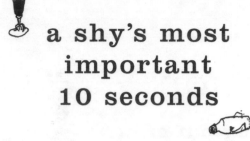

a shy's most important 10 seconds

No Need to Stay Zapped All Day

If you've faithfully been doing your morning 'demented duck on speed' exercise, high-octane energy will still be flowing through your veins by the time you get to work. However, if you try to maintain a super-cheerful, gung-ho personality all day, you'll be brought home on a stretcher. There are only a few strategic moments when you must re-pump up the enthusiasm from your morning exercise.

The old chestnut, 'You never have a second chance to make a good first impression' is splendid news for Shys. So is another: 'First impressions last practically for ever.' That means, if you pump it up and put pizzazz into your person-ality for a paltry 10 seconds when greeting someone, that memory takes a long time to fade. They'll think of you as one of the most beloved species, 'an energetic and opti-mistic' individual.

Why 10 seconds? That is the time it takes to make a first impression. Even the most lethargic among us can juice it up for that amount of time.

“ I'm basically a very quiet person and don't have much to say in a group. I work in a post office and there is a woman there who gives

everybody a big hello every morning. People like her a lot, so I thought I'd try it. I think they were surprised the first time I did it. I stayed with it, however, and I see people responding to me better although I'm just as quiet as I used to be."

TINA – CONCORD, NEW HAMPSHIRE

Come On Big

You are introduced to Archibald at a Chamber of Commerce meeting. 'Hello, Archibald, I'm so happy to meet you' are the words. But say them as though you had just won the lottery. Now that Archibald has pegged you as Mr or Ms Personality, he is more likely to interpret any ensuing silence as sincere interest in him.

SHYBUSTER 19:

Click on 'Animate' for 10 Seconds

Sure it's tough. But how bad can 10 seconds be? Any Shy can juice up the volume and press the 'animate' button for that long. These vibrant few seconds are a great kick off to a confident relationship.

" I started trying something last year that has worked very well for me. I give people a big smile and an enthusiastic hello. At first it sounded all fake to me but I saw others responding with a big smile so I continued. Because they're so friendly with me now I feel less self-conscious."

LAMONT – GLASGOW, SCOTLAND

who's the boss?
your mind or body?

If It Looks Like a Shy, Sounds Like a Shy, and Walks Like a Shy, It Must Be a Shy

Those of you who have read my other books know one of my most deeply-held beliefs. In fact, for me, it has reached the highly elevated state of an ideology, a dogma, tenant, gospel. It is – trumpet blare please – *Fake it til you make it.*

At first glance that probably seems like lightweight advice, the kind you'd find promulgated in such profound publications as *Cosmopolitan* or *Women's Own*. But it is wisdom for the ages.

Mother Nature created it. Ancient philosophers expounded on it. Gestalt principles confirmed it. Recently it has been carved in stone for the modern world, in more erudite words of course, by a research team with a grant from the Behavioral Science Division of the Ford Foundation.[1]

Your Mind-Body Battle for Togetherness

Your mind and your body instinctively strive to be in accord with each other. If they are not, you feel unbalanced.

Individuals strive to keep their cognitions psychologically consistent. When inconsistencies arise, they instinctively strive to restore consistence.[2]

When your mind thinks 'I am shy,' your body accommodates and acts shy. And when your body moves like it's shy, your mind says, 'I guess I'm shy.'

Here is your mind and body having one of their daily chats:

Your Mind asks your Body: *Hey, why are we slumping? What are you trying to tell me?*

Body answers: *I'm telling you, Brain, that we are shy.*

Mind: *Well, there certainly is a lot of physical evidence. I guess you're right, Bod. We are shy.*

Body: *Excuse me, Brain. Did I just hear you say we are shy?*

Mind: *Well, yes, Bod. Look how we slump and can't look people in the eye.*

Body: *Um, I guess you're right, Brain. OK, I'll accommodate you and move like a Shy. Maybe I'll even add a little blushing and stammering to be more convincing.*

Mind and Body in Unison: *Wonderful, then we'll be together again.*

In a bizarre sort of way, that satisfies you. Your mind and body agree. The mental health community calls it 'cognitive consistency' and human beings instinctively strive for it.

So how do you escape this Catch-22? You have two choices. The first is to convince your mind that you are not shy so your body behaves accordingly. This takes a long time on the psychiatrist's couch, lots of money, and maybe some pharmacotherapy or medication thrown in.

Choice two: Train your body to act confidently so your mind follows suit. This is what the experts recommend. It's a lot easier to whip your body into shape than your brain. You know all the basic stuff: Stand tall, look people in the eye, smile and speak up. *Start practising your SHYBUSTERs on the least intimidating people. Work your way up to the most difficult.*

The Goodbye-to-Shy Theme Song: Simple to Scary

The lyrics of this song are 'I'm starting with the simplest and working my way to the scariest.' You can put the song to your favourite music – classical, Country and Western, acid rock – as long as the lyrics are the same.

Sing the song to yourself as you do every SHYBUSTER in this book. Soon it will be tough to find *anyone* who intimidates you.

If you sing 'Simplest to Scariest' and go at your own pace, soon your mind will soon say to your body:

Mind: *Hey Bod, let's go to the party.*

Body: *Yahoo! I'm ready, Mind. Let's party!*

What Super-Sure Looks Like

A multitude of fascinating factors come under the 'looking confident 'umbrella. There isn't space here to explore the thousands of subtle signs that signal confidence. I cover them in my book *How to Talk to Anyone*. However, here are a few hints to tide you over. Self-assureds do the following things instinctively. You can do them consciously until they become second nature.

1. When you are at a gathering, do not stand close to the wall or by the snacks. Walk directly to the dead-centre of the room. That's where all the important people instinctively stand.

2. When you are going through a large door or open double doors, don't walk on one side. Walk straight through the middle. It signifies confidence.

3. At a restaurant, unless there is an established hierarchy, go for the seat at the end of the table facing the door. That is the power position.

4. Sit in the highest chair in a meeting or on the arm of the couch – but not higher than the boss!

5. Make larger, more fluid movements. Confident people's bodies occupy more space. Shys take as little as possible, as if to say, 'Excuse me for taking up this much of the earth.'

6. Keep your hands away from your face and never fidget.

7. When you agree with someone, nod your head up from neutral (jaw parallel to the floor), not down.

8. When walking towards someone and passing, be the last person to break eye-contact.

9. For men: Don't strut like a bantam rooster. But to look like a leader, swing your arms more significantly when you walk. When you are seated, put one arm up on the back of a chair. Occasionally lean back with your arms up and your hands behind your head.

10. For women: To seem self-assured, square your body towards the person you're talking to and stand a tad closer. Naturally, give a big smile *but* let it come ever so slightly so it looks sincere, not nervous.

SHYBUSTER 20:

Let Your Body Be the Boss

Whenever you catch yourself in that 'Beat me again, Master' body language, snap into the Master's position. When you move like a Sure all day long, your mind will begin to believe you already are one.

And, of course, need I even mention posture?

" I read somewhere that a negative mind-set causes negative body language, but that the opposite is true, too – you can alter your attitude by adopting a positive demeanour. I tried that, by at first simply forcing myself to walk upright and hold my head level – while still avoiding others' gazes. That did boost my confidence to a point where I could start looking at people, later on make and hold brief eye-contact, to the current point where about half the people I make eye-contact with break it first. "

KOOS Z. – PRETORIA, SOUTH AFRICA

how to make eye-contact easy

Get Comfortable Looking at Two Eyeballs per Person

'Make more eye-contact.' For Shys, that's like telling a vampire to make good eye-contact with the sun. *What if they want to stop and talk to me? What if I freeze up? What if they think I'm stupid? What if they see me blushing? What if ...? No, I'll just pretend I didn't see them.*

Sound familiar? Your eyes are a vital body part to start SOS (Stamping Out Shyness.)

Some well-meaning people advise, 'Look at people's eyebrows.' Do they really believe you can have a meaningful conversation with a pair of eyebrows? Or, 'Look at the bridge of their nose.' Sure, then they tell their friends you're cross-eyed. Tricks don't work.

There is no way around it. Shys *must* master good eye-contact.

If only we thought like the Chinese. To them, having no eye-contact is a sign of respect. But alas, we can't inject their cultural mores into Western culture and polish our shoes with our eyes while talking to the boss. Here we must have eye-contact commensurate with our culture – confident and spirited. Unfortunately when people see you avert your eyes, these are not the qualities that come to mind. It's more likely they'll think you shifty, shy, sneaky, snobbish, and possibly a liar.

" My worst year was my first year in high school. I was shy to the point where I couldn't look anybody in the eye. I always avoided looking at faces by looking down. So much so that I sometimes walked past my classmates without realizing it, because I was too afraid to look up. They thought I was snubbing them so I wound up not having any friends.**"**

SONJA – SEATTLE, WASHINGTON

During my shy years, or I should say decades, I tried the eyebrow thing, the bridge-of-the-nose thing, and a few other duds. I feared it was hopeless and I was sentenced to be one of the '13 per cent-ers', the ones who are lifelong Shys.

Baby, What Beautiful Eyes You Have

I am always amazed and impressed by the way babies handle eye-contact. Their tiny fearless eyes stare straight into mine. When they grab their little toes and squeal with delight, they don't worry about their feet being too big or too small. If I gently pat their little tummies they don't think I mean, 'Hey kid, gettin' a little chubby there, aren't cha?' They don't blame themselves for scarfing down that extra jar of pureed applesauce and peaches.

They feel they're pretty cool no matter what they look like. And they assume everyone else thinks they are, too. So they confidently keep gazing at me until they get bored.

'Ho hum,' they decide. 'Now I'll stare at some other silly adult face.'

“ In high school, I couldn't look a single person in the eye. In class I kept to myself and during breaks I would escape to the back of the school hall. Interaction with my peers virtually 'paralysed' me with fear.

Interestingly enough, I have little problem interacting with people much younger or older than I am – I am not too shy around kids or people approximately the age of my parents. But the closer someone gets to my own age, the more intimidating they are to be around.”

SCOTT – STURGIS, SOUTH DAKOTA

If you have a major problem making eye-contact with people (and what Shy doesn't?), start taking baby-steps. Looking into an infant's tiny little peepers starts you on your way.

SHYBUSTER 21:

Infant Eyes

I know 'staring a baby down' isn't quite like staring down a charging bull. However, strong eye-contact with the under-two set familiarizes you with the crucial 'eyeball-to-eyeball' game. Then slowly raise the stakes. Work your way up to the scale to tots, then children, then teens. Obviously, don't stare too long, but try it in short bursts.

After you have mastered making eye-contact with juvenile eyes, gradually work towards making eye-contact with people your own age. You may be able to make a smooth transition to this.

If, however, the eyeballs of contemporaries make you jittery, skip them for the moment, and jump to the top of the totem pole. You'll find it easy to make eye-contact with *much* older folks.

Start with the over-70 set – sitting on a bus, waiting in a queue, wherever and everywhere. Many old people, especially in large cities, feel neglected. Look right into their eyes, smile, and make them feel special.

SHYBUSTER 22:
Octogenarian Eyes

Leap to the summit of the spectrum and make eye-contact with the well over-70 set, then work your way down to the over-60s, etc. – until you can look comfortably into the eyes of people your own age.

" You asked for 'success stories' with shyness. I had a terrible time smiling and making eye-contact with people. So I started making eye-contact with people who didn't intimidate me. I looked at bus drivers when I got on the bus, cashiers when I bought something and waitresses when they served me something. The more used to that I got, the more I was able to make eye-contact with other people and people I knew. "

KENNETH – GLOUCESTER, ENGLAND

Raise the Bar

Now let's raise the bar on beginners' eye-contact. As soon as you've completed the 'Young Eyes/Old Eyes' exercises, take on some anonymous eyes, non-threatening ones, ones that expect and welcome your eye-contact.

Salespeople standing behind their counters in department stores have been told to smile at customers. Help them do their job! They are eager for your eye-contact. Rather than eye-balling strangers on a crowded street, try this ...

SHYBUSTER 23:
Eager Eyes

Walk through a department store and make brief eye-contact with every salesperson. Ladies, when you feel comfortable, stroll through the men's department and make eye-contact with the salesmen there. Gentlemen, when you can make eye-contact with the cosmetics girls, you'll know you've graduated from beginners' eye-contact.

As for all exercises in this book, monitoring never hurts. If you have a friend who knows you're shy, take them shopping with you. If you don't meet your target number of eye-contact 'hits', buy your buddy lunch.

Longer Eye-contact Made Simple

" I try to smile and make eye-contact with everyone because I know I should. But it is so painful to keep my eyes on someone else's. And sometimes I feel like I'm smiling at them like a hyena. My mind is racing a mile a minute and the temptation to finish my smile and look away is too big for me to resist. Once I tried counting to three, but it seemed so long. I don't want people to think I'm staring at them. But if I stop smiling and looking at them they think I'm unfriendly."

CLAIRE – BLOOMFIELD, VERMONT

The Unspoken 'I Like You'

Good idea, Claire, and I'd like to tweak it a tad. Claire's concept of counting to three is good, but repeating dull numbers does seem interminably long and does nothing for your smile.

Try this: After you've smiled, *silently* say 'I like you' to your eye-contact recipient. There are three advantages to this:

1. The time it takes for you to say to yourself 'I like you.' is precisely the amount of time your lingering eye-contact should last.
2. Saying the words silently gives you a warm expression. Unless you really work at it, your mind can't say 'I like you' while your face is saying 'You intimidate me' at the same time.
3. Your inner monologue keeps your mind from racing to other thoughts – like 'I wonder what they think of me?'

SHYBUSTER 24:
Say 'I Like You' Silently

While keeping eye-contact, say silently to yourself, 'I like you.' Now you're right on target with timing your eye-contact and smile. Soon it will become second nature and you can chuck this crutch.

a quick smile and a slow jet get you nowhere fast

Whoops, I Missed Your Smile Because I Blinked

Eye-contact without a slow smile is like a crackle without a pop. It has no effect at all. You can't just flash your teeth at someone and think you're done. How your smile feels from inside your cheeks can be very different from what other people see. You *feel* it's as wide as a watermelon. But to recipients it can look like a tiny crack in a plate.

" I didn't date very much but I had some good friends in college. When I moved to Boston for my first job, I was lonely and wanted to meet some women. I'd go to bars and clubs and smile at some attractive women but they'd never smile back so I never dated much there either.

Then I got transferred to LA. I love California. It's much more friendly than Boston for me. Women actually ask me to dance with them. I started going regularly to a club in Long Beach. One night a woman I was dancing with asked

me why I always looked so sad. I was
shocked and asked what she meant. She
said she'd been watching me for several
weeks and I always looked sad.
I remembered that several other people
had told me that over the years, too.
I decided to try to look happier because
maybe I looked sad even when I wasn't."

KEIL – LOS ANGELES, CALIFORNIA

Is the Smile You Give the Smile They Get?

I've never met Keil, but it sounds as though he *thought* he
was smiling but people didn't see it that way. You want to
make sure the smile you give is the smile they get.

All you need is a well-lit mirror – and a sense of humour
definitely helps. Now smile big. Smile small. Smile sexy. Smile
sad. Smile sarcastic. Smile scared.

Now go for a pretentious smile, then a phony smile. You
need to know how it feels *from the inside,* so you can be
sure you're not flashing those hideous smiles when you
mean them to be friendly.

Smile at Your Goldfish

Now, start smiling at your cat, dog or goldfish. Work your
way up to smiling at that sweet little elderly lady on the bus,
or the old codger who lives down the street. Not only are
these 'beginner's smiles' crucial in your anti-shyness campaign, but they give joy to everyone you smile at.
Remember, inside every wrinkled old lady lurks a beautiful

young girl. Inside every tattered old man lives a school football star. When you smile at them, they feel you're smiling at their inner selves. It's a win-win situation.

SHYBUSTER 25:
Make Faces at Yourself

Get to know your smile from the inside, outside, right and left. Feel the difference between grinning and grimacing. Know when you are leering like a lecher or smirking like a stalker. Only when you know how each feels can you polish yours to a confident, friendly and welcoming smile. (Hint: You'll know you've succeeded when you see your eyes getting into the act.)

Now it's time to take your smile-show on the road. First smile at people you don't find threatening. Work your way up to those who intimidate you slightly, say a colleague at work, or a nice-looking person you're attracted to. Keep smiling at scarier and scarier people.

Soon you'll be smiling at the scariest people – new acquaintances, your boss, even the drop-dead fantastic potential partner who used to make you forget your mother tongue was English.

for the want
of a smile

As a recovered shy, I'm now an incessant people-watcher. Whether I'm in an airport, a Starbucks, or at a gathering, my eyes sweep the room like an electronic scanner silently scrutinizing people's interactions. Often a man's and a woman's eyes meet. You can almost hear it. For them, the music is swelling and strains of 'Our Love is Here to Stay' fill the room.

But he's shy and quickly looks away as though he's not the least bit interested. She's timid too and inspects the floor for dust. Inevitably, after about 30 seconds, she risks a brisk peek to see if he's still looking at her. But alas, out of timidity, he is looking elsewhere. Another half-minute passes and, puffing up his courage and his chest, he now hazards another look. But alas, she is gone.

You've no doubt heard the expression 'For the want of a nail, a shoe was lost; for the want of a shoe, a horse was lost; for the want of a horse, a rider was lost; for the want of a rider, a battle was lost; for the want of a battle, a kingdom was lost. All for the want of a nail!'

SHYBUSTER 26:
A Lifetime of Happiness Was Lost

For the want of a smile, a conversation was lost. For the want of conversation, a date was lost. For the want of a date, a love was lost. For the want of love, a lifetime of happiness together was lost. All for the want of a smile.

Be the *first* to smile and say 'Hello.' It could change your life. Always have the courage to smile at someone you find attractive.

> " I am petrified of intimacy. I know that if I fall in love I will give myself so completely and I will be so vulnerable. A guy could walk all over me and I would just lie down and say 'Walk harder.' I would lose total control.
>
> Because of this I don't even look at nice guys whom I could love. I just date jerks because I know I'm not going to fall for them, so I feel safe. I hate what I'm doing but I can't stop it. It scares me that my soulmate might be smiling at me from across the room and I can't even smile back. "

DIANA – LINDENHURST, NEW YORK

snobs don't
smile either

> **"** Some people think of shy people as
> unfriendly, or as snobs.
>   This is not true. It is a very bad
> misunderstanding because most of us
> shy people care very much about other
> people. In my case it is because I am
> often so worried that what I say might
> be misinterpreted or hurt somebody, that
> I say nothing at all. **"**
>
> WENDY – LITTLE FALLS, MINNESOTA

A Case of Mistaken Identity

We know how people catch measles, what they feel like,
how long they last, and how to treat them. Nobody is going
to look at a face full of red speckles and say, 'What in the
world are those funny red spots?'

Shyness isn't so conspicuous. People don't know you're
dizzy, nauseous, numb and sweating like a hog in a sauna.
But they can think something worse. If you don't make eye-
contact and smile at people, they often misread shyness and
interpret it as snobbery.[1]

Who, Me? A Snob?

Think about it. Snobs don't acknowledge people first. Shys don't either. Snobs don't greet people with their names. Shys don't either. Snobs don't hang out with the gang. Shys don't either. So is it any wonder people might mistake a Shy for a snob?

If I'd known that in college, it would have saved me sleepless nights. In junior year, I had an all-consuming crush on a sexy-looking guy in my art class. He was French – from Paris yet. I envisioned Jacques riding on a bicycle wearing a beret and with a long French stick under his arm. I pictured us kissing under the Pont Neuf bridge on the banks of the River Seine. Somehow kissing under Garrison Avenue Bridge over the Arkansas River didn't hold the same glamour for me.

I loved the way he spoke. Ever since I was a pre-teen, foreign accents have made my knees go weak. But alas, all I could do was sneak shy surreptitious peeks at Jacques from behind my easel.

Right after art class, we both had Chemistry class on the other side of the campus. The instant the bell rang I'd swiftly stash my brushes and sprint across the campus. I was terrified that, if we walked together, I'd be speechless or say something stupid.

Once, during my usual breathless sprint, I heard footsteps running behind me, then a throaty French accent.

'Lili, Lili! Why ees it you are walking zo fast?'

I froze like a frightened ferret. Words crumbled on my parched tongue before they could tumble out.

He caught up with me and asked, 'Lili, we both go zees way every day but you never walk with me. You do not like me?'

'Uh, no. No no, I mean yes.'

'Voilà, it is settled then,' he said with feigned bravado. 'From today on, we will walk together to Chemistry class. Yes?' My heart was beating so fast, he must surely have heard the thumping. We strolled a few seconds in silence, him smiling and me screaming inside. Finally I was unable to halt the tears welling up in my eyes.

'Lili is somezing wrong?' he asked.

I could hold it back no longer. I blurted out, 'I am shy!'

'Excuse me, you zaid you are what?'

'Shy! Shy!' I sobbed.

He put his hand on my shoulder. 'Lili, I am zo happy now because I felt you were avoiding me because you did not like me. Excuse me for saying, but I thought you might be what you Americans call a snub.'

'A snub?' I managed to croak.

He laughed. 'Oh, no, I mean a snob.'

I couldn't believe it. Jacques thought I was stuck up!

> **Many people make the mistake of thinking Shys are stand-offish or feel they are better than others.[2]**

Good Looks Can Count Against a Shy

Good-looking Shys, you are much more at risk of people thinking you are arrogant. After all, they figure, if you are so stunning, the world is your oyster. Why should you even look at them?

❝ I suffered a great deal of misunderstanding when I was in college. I was blessed with good looks and many people mistook my timidity for overbearing arrogance and were insulted by it. The worst part was I actually knew this and tried to turn my image around. But I was terror-stricken about speaking to them. The blood would rush to my head and the power of speech completely failed me.❞

DARLENE – LOS ANGELES, CALIFORNIA

SHYBUSTER 27:
Don't Let Them Feel Snubbed

You've been telling yourself to yourself for years 'Don't act shy' because you know it's painful for you. But Shys are usually very nice people and don't want to hurt others. Turn that lens around and think of the other person. Tell yourself, 'I must look at other people and smile, for *their* sake, not mine. If I don't, they can think I'm ignoring and rejecting them.'

Shys, because you are more sensitive to others' feelings than most, make absolutely sure people don't feel you are slighting them. Try to put your shyness in the background for a moment. Greet people, smile and be as friendly as you can – for their sake, not yours!

I recently came across this poem by Alfred Lord Tennyson and cried as I read it. It is about a man named Edward Gray who was desperately in love with an Ellen Adair. But he mistook her extreme shyness as snubbing him. Devastated, he 'fled over the sea'.

Soon after he left, he heard that she had died. He returned and was grief-stricken when he learned that she had loved him intensely but was too timid to tell him. She died of love for him when he left. He sat by her grave and cried out ...

> Shy she was, and I thought her cold,
> Thought her proud, and fled over the sea;
> Fill'd I was with folly and spite,
> When Ellen Adair was dying for me.
>
> Ellen Adair she loved me well,
> Against her father's and mother's will;
> Today I sat for an hour and wept
> By Ellen's grave, on the windy hill.
>
> There I put my face in the grass –
> Whisper'd, 'Listen to my despair;
> I repent me of all I did;
> Speak a little, Ellen Adair!'

Then I took a pencil, and wrote
On the mossy stone, as I lay,
'Here lies the body of Ellen Adair;
And here the heart of Edward Gray!'

Bitterly wept I over the stone;
Bitterly weeping I turn'd away.
There lies the body of Ellen Adair!
And there the heart of Edward Gray!'

That was poetic fiction, but it's happening all over the world in real life.

" Another thing about my being a shy person and my relationships with women is that, in my life, I feel I've missed out on an opportunity to be with the person who could have been my soulmate.

I knew her in college. We were in the same Physics class. But I never had the courage to speak to her. Her name was Sandi.

However, I got to know Sandi a couple of years later when, by coincidence, she was working for the same agency I worked for. She was everything I could have wanted in a woman. She was indisputably attractive, intelligent, had a sense of humour and was very understanding. Naturally, I figured she had a boyfriend so I didn't ask her out.

Sandi went to another department and.
I saw her from time to time. Then she got
married.

A few months later Sandi and I were
talking in the hall and she told me she was
pregnant and that some of her office-mates
were having a little party for her, and she
invited me. We had a couple of drinks at the
party. We were sort of joking around and she
told me she'd always wanted me to ask her
out. I wanted to die right then and there.
Naturally, I can't help but think that if I
hadn't been so shy, I maybe could have
married her and it would be my baby she was
carrying. Now that chance is gone and I'll
never have a similar opportunity again."

RON – CHERRY HILL, NEW JERSEY

if at first you don't succeed, swear!

Three Strikes and You're *Not* Out

If you don't smile effortlessly right away and make comfortable eye-contact, simply swear to keep at it. Looking at people and smiling will soon be second nature. You'll be so thrilled with the way people react to you that you'll never suffer from what's called 'recidivism'. That often means going back to criminal ways and ending up in 'the slammer' again.

When I was 12, I was a three-time phone loser until I finally made it. Every time the phone rang it was my cue to dash down to the cellar or jump into the empty bathtub pretending to be having a bath.

'Answer it, dear,' Mama would say. I'd pretend not to hear her.

Objectively I realized how pathetic it was, a 12-year-old girl crouching in the tub fully clothed and shivering like a sick kitten. Every night I prayed, 'Please, dear God, don't make me afraid of talking on the phone anymore.' Then one night I dreamed I was cowering in the empty tub again. Suddenly the bathroom walls trembled. As though there were a speaker in every tile, I heard a deep voice in Dolby surround-sound: 'My child, I only help those who help themselves.'

Thinking back now, it should have been, 'You lily-livered little twit, get your tush out of the tub and answer the phone!' In any case, I woke up in a cold sweat.

The next morning I descended the staircase feeling like a saint following God's divine calling. As I picked up the receiver, ready to make a call, the cord suddenly looked like a coiled poisonous black snake. I screamed, dropped the phone and ran to my bedroom.

My tears turned to anger. And my anger turned to rage against myself. I went back to tackle the beast again. I dialled the first seven digits that came to mind. Then quickly hung up.

I tried again. Ring ... I hung up.

I tried again. Ring ... Ring ... Ring ...

No one home. I breathed a sigh of relief and walked away feeling I had succeeded.

In fact, I had! Even though I hadn't completed one call, I was on the right track.

SHYBUSTER 28:
Your First Failure Is Success

Early failure is not confirmation you can't do it. Do not crawl back into your shell and feel you are destined to dwell there for ever.

The first failure, the second, and even the third are all steps to your eventual success – so long as you keep trying.

I'm sure you've heard the phrase, 'It's not whether you win or lose, it's how you play the game.' If you tackle eye-contact and smiling or any other tough situation and fail, don't be discouraged. Take a deep breath and vow to succeed before the sun sets.

66 **When I was a kid we lived in Florida. I didn't have any friends because I was too shy. But there were lots of flat streets and I got real good at roller-skating. I loved it. Then we moved to a town in Arizona where there was no place to skate but there was a roller-rink. But I was too shy to go because people would look at me. I went a couple of times but couldn't take it so I stopped.. I didn't skate for about a year and was miserable. Finally I forced myself and I'm so glad I did, because I'm in the Arizona Roller Derby Surly Gurlies. And you can't be shy there! Persistence paid off.** 99

BABS – CHANDLER, ARIZONA

Telephone Round Two: I made some simple calls: the grocery store to ask their hours, the bus station to ask the schedule, the department store to ask if they had a certain brand of slippers.

Round Three: By the end of the next week I was ready to make a real call. My cherished little Siamese cat Louie had been acting sluggish. I phoned the vet and made an appointment.

Louie lived a long and happy life. That was my reward for conquering phone fear.

" It is not important you do it now. It is important that you envision and will someday do it."
GEORGE BALANCHINE

Let that someday be tomorrow. No later.

battling blushing, sweating and clammy hands

What If You Know You Can't Hide It?

> **"** If I go out to dinner with friends or co-workers, and everyone is having a conversation, I don't take part a lot of times because I am afraid I am going to blush. Another problem is I have been dating my boyfriend for over a year now, and I will not take my clothes off in front of him in the light. He always complains about that but I cannot help it. I am blushing when he undresses me and I don't want him to see it. **"**
>
> LESLEY – BRISTOL, ENGLAND

Some Shys sweat, blush or exude other overt signs of shyness, so they figure they have to tell people they are shy. Not necessarily. Sometimes sweat is just sweat. Sometimes a blush is just a blush.

But if you get red and soggy excessively and are 100 per cent positive that it will be obvious, here's the solution.

Hit It on the Head with Humour

This is easy to do because some Sures blush, sweat or have wet paws, too. Before shaking hands you can joke, 'Wait a minute, let me wipe it off first or you're not going to like what you feel' or 'Shake at your own risk. My hands are *always* sopping.' Highlight the 'always' and they won't even connect it with shyness. (Home remedy hint: Try a little antiperspirant and a dusting of powder.)

One of my clients is a profligate blusher, yet an extremely confident managing director. Local television often invites Bernard to comment on the state of the economy. Being on TV is an intense blush-generating situation for him. Bernard knows he's going to be delivering his interview with a crimson face. But when he blushes, he is not the least flustered by it. He even seems to enjoy people teasing him about it.

Here Comes Bernie the Blusher

Each time he arrives at the station for an interview, the man at the welcome desk pushes the intercom to announce: 'Calling all make-up artists. Calling all make-up artists. Girls, get the extra pancake (cover-up make-up). Bernie Blush is here.'

He joins their laughter as people greet him in the hall, 'Hi there, Red!' 'How's it going, Rosy?' They're not bothered by it because they know he's not either. Unselfconsciously Bernard has warned people that he might blush at any moment. He chuckles, 'Don't take it personally!' Sometimes he'll joke, 'My wife hates having hot flushes, so I'm having them for her.'

Bernard proudly calls himself the world's expert on blushing. Here are a few esoteric facts he told me – which would only be of interest to fellow-blushers: Blushing runs in families, but babies don't blush. Fifty-one per cent of people blush and many of them are not shy.[1] Women blush more than men, and people of all skin colours blush.

Bernard pretends to be jealous of his assistant managing director, Jolan, a Native American. 'He blushes worse than I do,' he grumbles. 'You just can't see it!'

SHYBUSTER 29:
Laugh It Off *Before* It Happens

If you have a shyness symptom that you know will obviously show, lightheartedly 'warn' people of your incipient blush, mushy mits or sweat flushes. No need to even mention shyness.

section VI

absolutely no-pain, lots-of-gain techniques

the power
and pleasure of
anonymity

Not So 'Merry Christmas' for a Shy

Every year our school had a Christmas pageant. It was a very
big deal. Adoring parents, relatives and friends of adoring
parents and relatives flocked to the school hall to see our
spectacular production. In the cast there were of course the
customary stars, Mary, Joseph, three wise men and a life-size
baby doll wrapped in swaddling clothes. To give everyone a
chance to participate our extravaganza also overflowed
with angels, shepherds, rabbits, cows, donkeys, horses,
goats and various burlap-swathed liggers from Bethlehem.
Appropriately enough, I was cast as a rabbit. Needless to say,
I was a scared little rabbit.

In typical theatrical tradition, a few budding actresses
dreamed of killing their classmates for these holy roles. But
I wanted to be as invisible as possible. My choice role would
be the Holy Ghost under a sheet.

Rehearsals terrified me and I refused to go on stage
unless I could wear my bunny mask. The teacher agreed,
telling the others that it helped me 'get into character'.
With this bogus anonymity I hopped around the stage on all
fours and gave an occasional quiet little 'chee chee' – the
sound, Mama told me, that rabbits make.

The night of the big bash came. Right alongside of the
confident cows, donkeys, horses and goats, I got through

the performance as a self-assured rabbit.

But there was a last-minute twist in the tale. We hadn't rehearsed the final bow. To thunderous applause, we all instinctively held hands or paws and came to the front of the stage. As we bowed in unison, all the other animals took off their masks and smiled proudly at the clapping crowd. Since I didn't take mine off, the donkey bowing next to me reached up and pulled it off.

No longer anonymous, I freaked out and covered my face with my paws. Much to my humiliation, and to the hilarity of the applauding audience, I ran off stage.

"Last summer I worked for a catering company and we all wore costumes like old-fashioned butlers, cooks and maids. Mine was a little French maid's outfit with a short skirt with ruffles and high heels. I was so surprised to realize that I didn't feel my usual shyness even dressed like that! I guess because when we were catering a party I didn't know anybody and, in that getup, probably nobody would recognize me anyway. It was so un-me."

EILA – BRISBANE, AUSTRALIA

I'm not asking you to walk around the mall wearing a mask, but do consider the proven remedial effect of temporary anonymity. It helps Shys face fearful situations that they will eventually have to face as themselves. When you are unidentified you have more courage to interact with people. That interaction, although anonymous, gives you experience communicating with people you might normally be shy around.

Temporary anonymity is an excellent step for the extremely shy.[1]

The Masked Shy

Philip Zimbardo, the man who is at the forefront of shyness research, employed the anonymity technique to help his extremely shy little brother recover. George was so shy that, like me, he hid if anyone came to the house. He was miserable at school, didn't make any eye-contact, and never played with the other kids.

His older brother Philip suggested that George might enjoy a special game, wearing a paper bag over his head with eyes and a mouth cut out. In fact, George liked it so much he wanted to wear the paper bag to school. The teacher agreed, saying she would tell the other students it was for fun. When the other students asked George who he was, he would proudly say 'Mr Nobody'.

This anonymity got him through the year playing unselfconsciously with the other kids. He was even able to be in the yearly circus production wearing it. The masked-man technique worked so well that, the following year, he performed one of the lead roles – without his face covered.

By the time George was in high school he had developed several close friendships. In his senior year, he was elected to class office.

" I'm a pretty big guy, 5'11 and 220 pounds.
That makes it all the worse being shy.
A buddy of mine owns a disco and one
night I get this call from him saying his
bouncer didn't show up and would I fill in.
I did and I didn't feel shy at all that night.
People thought of me as 'the bouncer' that
night, not as Freddie. I've filled in a
couple of weekends since then and I
think it's helped. "

FRED – BALTIMORE, MARYLAND

My Costumed Caper

Even before research confirmed the efficacy of anonymity in remedying shyness, I did something similar when I was teaching nursery school.

One Halloween, the head-teacher asked some of the teachers to take the kids trick-or-treating. But knocking on strangers' doors and having to make small-talk while they dumped M&Ms into the kids' bags was too much for me. While fantasizing the horror of it all, I remembered my Christmas pageant and what a confident masked rabbit I was.

I went to a costume shop and bought, you guessed it, a rabbit mask. Once or twice, during our trick-or-treating, I even took it off when talking with a stranger. I felt vulnerable at those unmasked moments, and still had difficulty making eye-contact. But the bottom line was, the next year I was able to take the kids trick-or-treating without hiding behind a mask.

" I used to be quite shy and not want to talk to people. But having been a professional clown over the summers of my college years, I don't think I'm allowed to use the title anymore. "

ROBERT – JACKSON, TENNESSEE

the out-of-town caper

Excuse Me, I'm a Stranger in Town

We could rename this section, 'Excuse Me, I'm Not from Round Here So I Can Make an Absolute Donkey of Myself and Nobody Will Give a Damn.' But that's a bit long for a title.

I'm not suggesting you walk around the mall with a paper bag on your head like little George, or chat with colleagues masked as a rabbit. There is a related, but saner way to practise social skills anonymously.

Start by listing the social situations you find difficult. Suppose your inventory looks something like this:

1. Asking strangers questions on the street
2. Shopping and not buying something for fear I'll disappoint the salesperson
3. Making eye-contact and smiling at people I don't know
4. Getting into extended small-talk with a stranger
5. Having an unpleasant or confrontational conversation.

Tuck the list into your pocket or purse and travel to a nearby town where there's zip, nada, zero chance anybody knows you. Pull the list out and start following it.

Ask five people on the street for directions. (If it helps, carry a map and a confused expression to make it more convincing.)

Continue down your list. *Try on three pairs of shoes at each shoe store in town and don't buy any of them.* That's good for a couple of hours.

Go to a department store and smile at every salesperson you pass. Pretend to be shopping and ask about different items in the store.

Get product recommendations – ask the pharmacist which is the best cream for poison ivy. Do it at every pharmacy in town.

When you're having lunch, *have the server describe the various dishes to you.* That's a good five minutes if you stretch it out.

Take a bus ride and talk to the person sitting next to you. That's about 10 minutes. Transfer to another bus and do the same. And another.

Here's a toughie but a goodie: *Buy an item in a store and ask about their returns policy. If it's liberal, return the item a couple of hours later.*

Add another hour or two of scary stuff and, if I've done the maths correctly, you'll have had five full hours of constant communicating. After that much talking in another town, how much you wanna bet it's going to be a lot easier to talk to people in your own town the next day?

SHYBUSTER 30:

Be Anonymous for a Day

Of course you are self-conscious about people making judgements about you. But, if they don't know you from Adam or from Eve, so what? You'll probably never see them again, so why should you care what they think of you? Like all the SHYBUSTERs, this one is tough. But, once you've done it a few times, you'll be astounded how your comfort level rises with people who previously intimidated you.

" I always shop at this one tacky department store where my sister works. (I hope she doesn't read this letter.) The reason is I'm embarrassed to go to a nice store and ask to see some things because I might not want any of them. Several times I've bought something I didn't want just because I didn't want to hurt the salesperson's feelings. My sister always takes me around her store and I feel more comfortable looking at things when she's doing the talking with the other salespeople she knows. "

DARLA – BEAVER, PENNSYLVANIA

SHYBUSTER 31:
Be an Undercover Shy

Take advantage of any situation where you can be relatively anonymous. Halloween parties or other events where you can wear a costume, of course, are ideal. But so are situations where you have a role other than being yourself – like bouncer or caterer. Volunteering at events to be 'the ticket-taker', 'the car-parker', the 'anything-but-totally-me' is a big boost.

dress as your fantasy person

You Feel Like What You Wear

While you're at it, get comfortable with very un-Shy clothing. Everybody goes to their wardrobe in the morning and asks themselves, 'Let's see, how do I feel today? What shall I wear?' People wear clothing commensurate with their self-image.

The MD of a major corporation feels he should be respected, so he pulls out his dark suit. A woman, when she wants to feel sexy, snatches a hot dress to reveal her assets. And kids who think they're cool wear whatever the other kids who think they're cool are wearing.

Just like everyone else, you go to your wardrobe in the morning and ask yourself the same question, 'How do I feel today?'

I ran a computer-search for the words 'I feel' through the e-mails I've received from Shys. Sadly, I found 'I feel dull.' 'I feel foolish.' 'I feel stupid.' 'I feel inferior.' 'I feel worthless.' 'I feel like a side-show freak.'

So, standing in front of your wardrobe each morning, you are *subconsciously* saying, 'Let me find some clothes that make me look dull, foolish, stupid, inferior, worthless or make me feel like a side-show freak.' Your hands instinctively go for dull duds – and naturally, you are judged on the way you dress.

Wear 'Look at Me' Clothes

The solution? Recapture the imagination and spirit of fun kids have when they play dressing-up. 'I want to be a princess.' 'I want to be a pirate.' 'I want to be a policeman.' So the princess, pirate and policeman costumes are tugged out of the trunk.

Do the same. Reaching for your daily gear, say to yourself 'I feel confident today.' Grab garments like your favourite Sures wear. Better yet, dress with flair or fun. Wear something that makes people turn and look at you.

Anything goes these days. Men, you've always wanted to wear a cape like Jean Valjean in *Les Miserables*? Women, you admire girls with perfect pedicures and sexy little strappy high-heeled sandals? Go for it!

> **❝ Let's face it, a suit and a nice pair of shoes can work wonders in how we are going to feel in any social situation. I really think investing in a good wardrobe is going to boost someone's confidence. Why do you think James Bond always wears a suit? ❞**
> DAMITRI – ATHENS, GREECE

Of course it doesn't have to be a suit. But Damitri is being faithful to his self-image, and that's what we all should aim for.

SHYBUSTER 32:
Kick Out the Dull Kit

Imagine the type of person you'd like to be –
Flamboyant? Happy-go-lucky? Professional? Punk?
Glamorous? High-class?

God bless freedom. Today you can be anybody
you want to be. Picture your desired image. Now, go
buy the outfit to match!

" My husband and I have been married for 18
years. Last July we went out to dinner and,
as usual, I was wearing a blouse that
covered me up. They had outdoor tables and
we were sitting at one. Underneath my
blouse I was wearing a bra and slip, and it
got so hot I unbuttoned the top few buttons.
My husband looked at my cleavage and I
thought his eyes were going to pop out. He
said, 'Honey, those are some boobs. Why do
you keep them covered up all the time?' I
don't know what got into me but I slipped
off my blouse and nobody noticed because
'slip tops' were in style. But my husband
sure noticed it. When we got home that
night, we made love for the first time with

the lights on and I didn't feel self-conscious at all. He was so hot that it turned me on, and now I go around the house in just my slip and bra sometimes, and I bought some sexier clothes. It really helped my self-image. I don't feel anywhere near as shy about my body as I used to. I even like going out dressed sexy."

DONNA – PORT HURON, MICHIGAN

Go Donna!

fries with that?

How Can I Help You?

Now we graduate from being 'totally anonymous' to 'almost anonymous'. An excellent (and profitable!) way to feel comfortable with people is to get a part-time job where you interact with the public. In high school and college, I worked as a cashier in a pharmacy, as shampoo girl in a hair salon, waitress in a greasy spoon, and an office temp. These experiences helped tremendously. Best of all, it wasn't that uncomfortable because I wasn't being judged on my personality or looks. I was being viewed as the anonymous cashier, shampoo girl, waitress, and temp. I think it helped me decrease my shyness from agonizing to acute.

" I've dealt with extreme shyness throughout my childhood and adolescence. It wasn't until I entered college and started working in a part-time job as a sales associate in a retail store that I finally confronted my shyness head-on. Getting out there and 'selling' pretty much forced me to step out of myself and converse with customers. The retail chain had an organized, standardized approach, which included asking questions

to 'qualify the customer' – that is, find out what needs/wants they have and which product would best satisfy these needs/wants. For me, that was very helpful interaction.**"**

BEN – CLARKSVILLE, TENNESSEE

SHYBUSTER 33:
Be a Part-time Job-hopper

Even getting a part-time job that forces you to say something as simple as 'D'you want fries with that?' a hundred times a day makes it easier to say 'Hi' to people you're not selling fast food to.

section VII

get a (new) life

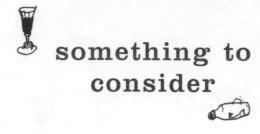

something to consider

Revelation on the Potty

When I was teaching nursery school, I loved confidently walking into the classroom and being greeted by a sea of happy little expectant faces. Now, I do realize that being confident around four- and five-year-olds is not an achievement of major magnitude, but I was very comfortable in that job.

There was, however, a problem. I began to talk like my students. The only time I mingled with adults was the third Monday of the month at school governors' meetings. During one of these I had to go to the lavatory. As I was standing up, I said, 'Excuse me, I have to go to wee wee.'

I could hear muffled tittering as I headed for the 'potty'.

That did it. Right there in the loo, I decided to quit teaching at the end of the semester and enter 'the adult world'. Being around the under-seven set was doing nothing for my shyness. I was in a happy rut as a nursery school teacher, and I knew I had to move on if I were going to achieve one of my greatest goals – relief from the pain of shyness.

If you are miserable big-time over your shyness, it's time to ask some serious questions like, 'Is my 9-to-5 life exacerbating my shyness? Is it work beneath my capability? Could I get a job more in sync with my life goals?'

My answer to the above questions were 1) Yes, 2) Yes, 3) Yes. It was time for me to move on.

SHYBUSTER 34:

Time to Jump Ship?

If your present job does not satisfy your goals, utilize your talents, alleviate your shyness or fulfil any other of your needs except that for money, consider exploring other options. (P.S. It's best to secure the lifeboat before taking the dive.)

Unfortunately I didn't follow my own advice of securing another job before bailing out. After the last day of term I stepped out of my job and joined the ranks of the unemployed with no lifeboats in sight. To top it off, job interviews terrified me. But I knew that by the following autumn I'd have to be working or I'd be out on the streets – and I was far too shy to beg!

I wangled a few job appointments. They all asked me the same questions. I couldn't tell them what really ran through my mind before grappling with a corporate-sounding answer:

When they asked, 'What are your strengths and weaknesses?' my secret truth was:

I love little kids but I'm unbearably shy around adults.

'Where do you want to be in five years?'

Not shy!

'Describe a challenge you met by taking a different approach.'

Sometimes if a kid doesn't want to eat their spinach, I swirl the spoon and pretend it's an airplane flying into their mouth.

'Tell me about a situation when you had to learn something complicated in a short time.'

I had to learn how to put a Mickey Mouse mobile together before my class began.

I soon realized that reading Mother Goose stories, ducking a water gun and chasing 20 kids around a playground hadn't prepared me for life in the fast track.

the shy's sneaky way to get a super job

The Professional World Cheats Shys

Perhaps one of the most devastating lifetime consequences of being shy is not getting a rewarding job which utilizes your talents. Sadly, it is often due to job-interview jitters Shys are slower to find a satisfactory job and their careers are more unstable right on through life.[1]

Unfortunately, most lifetime Shys work at a job which is far below their capabilities. In fact, a study published in the *Journal of Vocational Behavior* called 'Inhibited Career Development: Testing the Unique Contribution of Shyness' substantiated this:

Most lifetime Shys work at a job which is far below their capabilities.[2]

'No Job' Stress

After half-a-dozen interviews, the stress from not hearing 'You're hired' made me jittery. Another six and I felt like a cockroach on a griddle. However, I discovered an interesting advantage to interviewing with many companies. Each interview became easier, and I soon realized why. All the interviewers asked practically the same questions.

I suspect all Human Resources professionals attend the same 'How to Intimidate Applicants' seminar. First they warm you up with casual questions, maybe even offer you coffee. Then, just when you're feeling all cozy, they lean back, squint their eyes and start shooting so-called 'insightful' questions at you.

Shys, get a book on what interviewers ask. Better yet, save your money. You'll find their hackneyed 'trick questions' all over the web.

The actual questions, however, are only part of the job interview experience. You've heard the standard advice for job hunters: 'Practise with your friends or family.' The heck with that. Go one step further, as I inadvertently did. Shys, here's the plan – cheat!

Get a Great Job by Cheating

I exaggerate. It is not exactly cheating. It is simply a deliciously devious way to get the job you deserve. First, get interviews with five or six companies you wouldn't dream of working for.

Interview with Company One will be terrifying.

Interview with Company Two will be scary.

Interview with Company Three will be intimidating.

But by Company Four, you're wise to their game. After a few more dry runs with companies you don't want to work for, you are prepared for your dream-job interrogation.

SHYBUSTER 35:

Interview with Companies You *Don't* Want to Work For

Sure, study up on the basic job-interviewer's trick questions. But to make sure you get the job you deserve, interview with half-a-dozen companies you don't want to work for. When you feel you know their game, go for the gold, the job you want.

Money Slips Through Shy Fingers

Shys, if you work for yourself, there is another professional reason you must shed your shyness. It's a law of gravity. Money sips through unassertive fingers.

> " I'm an estate agent and deal with people daily to some degree. I have been struggling in this career for three years now. I know it is not the best career choice for someone who is shy, but I enjoy helping people and I enjoy the property field. However, shyness has cost me new clients and has lost me opportunities. One guy had been trying unsuccessfully to sell his house for some time. He met me at an open house and

invited me over. We chatted briefly, and I got out as quickly as I could because I was nervous. I didn't know what to say or even how to be friendly. Two days later he had listed his home with another agent who made $18,000 on the deal. Being shy has cost me easily thousands in potential income, if not hundreds of thousands. In fact, I have a lead now from a woman looking for a million-dollar house (approximately $23,000 potential commission) and I am scared to death to call her."

DAVE – PROVIDENCE, RHODE ISLAND

During this corporate quest I found my thoughts wafting back to a teenage fantasy of being a flight attendant. In those days, flight attendants didn't have to hawk headsets or keep the peanuts-per-passenger ratio as low as possible. Those were also the days when 'airline food' was not an oxymoron.

The more I thought about it, the more ideal it seemed. Shyness was my greatest challenge and this was the answer – even better than the corporate world I'd gone after. On the plane I'd have to deal with planeloads of grown-up passengers – saying 'Hello, Welcome,' then 'Goodbye, thanks for flying with us' maybe a hundred times in a row.

Pan American Airways was my dream. However, after the inspiration hit about interviewing with companies I didn't want to work for, I interviewed with American, United, TWA and a few other now-defunct airlines first. By the time I went to Pan Am, I knew their most important qualification – a perpetual smile. I went in grinning like a chipmunk and got the job.

section VIII

parties and other places in hell

building up
to bashes

The Party-a-Thon

After six weeks of living in barracks at JFK Airport I 'got my wings'. That was our proud parlance for graduating from flight-attendant training. Like most of the new stewardesses (as people called us in the days before we got all politically correct and said 'flight attendants'), I was broke. As a result, most of us cooped up with several other 'stews' in a block of flats near the airport. 'The Stew Pound', as legions of aspiring suitors called it, was infamous for nightly parties. I never dreamed I'd end up living in a non-stop party-a-thon.

My roommates were two drop-dead gorgeous Scandinavians, Annika and Ulla, which didn't do much for my confidence. Naturally, like any building housing a bevy of beauties, herds of hopeful men swarmed round it like bees to honey. Sadly, many ended up fried like insects in a bug-zapper. As much of a seller's market as it was, I was too shy to talk even to the grilled ones.

Since the flats were smaller than the training centre toilets, the parties spilled out into the hall. In spite of their relative poverty, the new stews could afford to be lavish hostesses because the parties were MBTB (Men Bring the Bottles) bashes – as well as the crisps, the dips and the pretzels.

Every night they weren't on a flight, Annika and Ulla's ears would perk up at sounds of music and clinking glasses. With a splash of perfume and a dash of lipstick, they'd be gone. I was rapidly running out of feeble excuses to stay home.

One December evening Annika was looking over our flight schedules. 'Oh, look at this. We're all going to be in town Thursday after next.'

'Let's give a Yulefest,' Ulla chimed in. 'What do you think, Leil?'

'Uh, what's a "Yulefest"?'

She laughed. 'A Christmas party!'

Drat, I knew this was going to happen sooner or later. 'Wonderful idea!' I said. I tried to calm my nerves by buying a dynamite dress for the party.

The dreaded night arrived. About 6.30, my roommates were excitedly helping each other with buttons, zips and make-up. I sat on my bed next to my new dress trying to hide my wet palms.

Annika looked at me. 'Leil, aren't you getting dressed?'

'Uh, well, I have a good friend who has a bad cold,' I lied. Mumbling something about taking her chicken soup I ran out, my beautiful new dress still spread out on the bed.

That night, sitting alone in a Chinese restaurant, I was miserable. Not only had I avoided a party, but I was letting my room-mates down, not helping out. And to top it off I'd lied to get out of it.

Party Like a Pigeon

Don't worry. I'm not going to pummel you with unhelpful 'advice' like 'Just force yourself to go to the party.' Shys must ease into it. You can't just submerge yourself and expect not to drown.

Have you ever been in the park feeding pigeons? You throw a few breadcrumbs on the path. Pigeons fly out of nowhere and land about 12 feet away. In time, one brave bird bolts towards a crumb, grabs it in his beak and flies away. The other pigeons see that their feathered friend survived the experience. You throw more crumbs and more pigeons make tentative approaches. As their confidence grows, their distance from you diminishes.

You go the next few mornings – same time, same place, same cuisine, same pigeons. Soon they're landing on your arm begging to eat out of your hand.

Take a hint from the pigeons. Go to the party, but stay 10 minutes max. Leave *before* you start to get uncomfortable. This helps you disconnect the words 'discomfort' and 'party' in your mind. Do NOT say to yourself, 'I should go to the party.' Say, instead, 'I'll spend 10 minutes there, that's all.' Then leave! Don't let the party get to the point of painful for you.

How painful can 10 minutes be? You could survive 10 minutes of the dentist drilling your teeth. But if he or she said, 'Don't worry, I'm only going to keep drilling for three hours,' you'd be running down the street with your dentist's bib still round your neck.

SHYBUSTER 36:
Prescription: One Small Dose of Party

Never avoid a party unless you have a note from your doctor. But stay only a short time. Then stay longer at the next. Longer at the next. And so on. Graduated exposure is the prescription.

Jeremy, who wrote this letter, definitely would have bene-fited from this SHYBUSTER:

" I know parties are a major meeting place. I'd like to have a relationship with a woman. But the idea of me striking up a relationship with a woman at a party is like science fiction because parties give me the jitters and I don't like the kind of woman who goes to a bar just to meet men. A friend of mine invited me to go to a party recently and I wasn't accustomed to mingling. I tried to stick with him but he was getting irritated that I was hanging on. I stayed for an hour after he told me to get lost but I got more miserable by the minute and finally left. At this rate I'll never meet anyone. "
JEREMY – MELBOURNE, AUSTRALIA

going to a party is not 'going to a party'

Don't Growl at the Guests

Ladies, if you spot a little kitten in the park curled up with a big mama-cat, it takes a tough woman indeed to resist approaching the small family, petting the mother and then, depending on Mum's demeanour, pick up kitty and cuddle it.

However, if Mama-cat transmogrifies herself into a satanic feline with narrow eyes and arched back, you change your mind about petting kitty.

Shys, at a party you obviously don't hiss at the other guests. But many of you do something equally effective when it comes to keeping people away. You often slump, look glum and fold your arms. That position is not exactly a welcome mat.

There is no need to repeat the simple stuff: Have good posture, eye-contact, body language that says 'I'm sure of myself' and say 'Hello, my name is ...' Don't let yourself fall back into a demeanour that shouts, 'I'd rather be in Siberia.'

> " I was very tall for a girl, 6'1 and, since I was shy, I hated my height. I got into the habit of slumping and, although I would force myself to go to parties, no one ever asked me out. One time a girlfriend of mine told

148

me not to slump so much. I caught a reflection of myself in the mirror and she was right. I felt much better and less shy when I stood up straight. From then on, I have asked my friend to help me with my posture and poke me every time she sees me slumping.**"**

HAYLEY – EDINBURGH, SCOTLAND

SHYBUSTER 37:
Have a Buddy Monitor You

Have a mate check your body language. Are you a 'Welcome' or 'No Trespassing' sign? If you slump, give your friend authorization to knuckle you in the back, just like your parents did to punish bad posture.

Be careful, though. Just showing up at a gathering without rehearsing your social skills is *not* a SHYBUSTER. If you look as tense as a turkey before Thanksgiving, it's no help. Mental health professionals have a name for nervous habits such as averting your eyes, speaking rapidly or clenching your hands to hide your trembling. They call it 'safety behaviours'. Unless you are a highly trained secret agent, you can't hide your insecurity completely. Professional body-language court witnesses call it 'emotional leakage'.

A study with a name almost as long as the point it makes confirms it: 'The Role of In-situation Safety Behaviors by Socially Anxious Subjects'.[1]

By using safety behaviors to 'play it safe' in social situations, socially anxious individuals found that ... they could not perform adequately without the safety behaviors.[2]

SHYBUSTER 38:
Showing Up Is Not Enough

Just depositing your bod in the middle of the bash is not 'going to a party'. Don't give yourself anti-shyness Brownie points unless you keep your body language friendly and you take the initiative in conversations. Ten minutes at the party practising your social skills is way better than staying an hour and being miserable. In fact, the latter is downright destructive because it reinforces your fear of parties.

" I used to force myself to go to parties, but arrive late so I could disappear in the crowd. One thing that helped me get over being allergic to parties was to go early. That way I was forced to talk to people because there would be so few there. "

IAN – BALTIMORE, MARYLAND

Not a bad idea, Ian! An additional advantage to arriving early is, as the party progresses, you now know a few people. You can hang with them a bit or join them later and they'll introduce you to other party-goers. That's easier than making a 'cold call' on someone standing nearby.

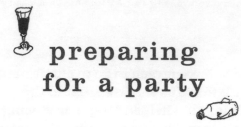

preparing for a party

My 'D'uh' Moment

Coming back from a party recently I had a blinding flash of the obvious. After all these years, the light bulb finally went off. Practically *all* of the conversations at the party were about the same old stuff: Movies. Marriage. Kids. Cats. Dogs. Holidays. Sport. The latest national disaster. Some of the party-goers ventured into more learned subjects such as books or the big bang theory of the universe. But basically it was all mundane and very predictable.

Put my dazzling discovery together with the fact that Shys, especially HSSs, take longer to frame their thoughts and, voilà! You have the next SHYBUSTER.

Make a mental list of all the possible subjects that could come up. Don't wait to frame your thoughts on Mr Celebrity Heartthrob and Ms Sexy Model's third divorce. Formulate your philosophy on this earth-shattering event now. If you wait to do it on the spot, by the time you open your mouth the gang is dishing some other dirt.

SHYBUSTER 39:
Ponder *Before* the Party

You don't need to ponder erudite subjects or plan polemic worthy of a university debating team. Simply be prepared to discuss the headlines of the day, local politics, who's doing what with whom, yada yada yada. If you gather your thoughts on these traditional topics before the gathering, you can jump into the conversation more quickly and more confidently.

While you're at it, prepare yourself for the inevitable banal interrogation:

'Wha' d'ya do last weekend?

'How's your Mum (Dad/kids/brother/sister/spouse/budgie, etc.)

'Where are you going on holiday this year?'

Plan energetic, enthusiastic and effervescent answers for their inquiring minds.

Go Ahead. Be Biased. (In a Politically Correct Way, Of Course)

You've heard people complaining that someone is 'too opinionated'? Don't worry. That's probably not your problem.

Most Shys are not opinionated enough. That fact gives you unrestricted licence to be just that.

SHYBUSTER 40:

Get Opinionated!

It's not enough to know 'they're rioting in Africa, they're starving in Spain, there are hurricanes in Florida and the southwest needs rain.' Have a clear conviction. Don't wait for someone to ask your thoughts on the matter. Formulate and update yours every day so you can dive into discussions like a Sure, without waiting for a formal invitation.

getting legless
is not the answer

Shys and Booze

A few years ago I was visiting a friend in my old home-town for the 4th of July weekend. While relaxing on Reenie's porch, a strikingly beautiful redhead came out the door across the street.

Reenie looked over at her.

'Wow, she's very beautiful,' I said.

'Yes,' Reenie agreed, 'But she's a witch. That's witch with a capital "B".'

'Why?'

'She's such a snob. If I say "Hi" to her she just looks the other way. I don't know anything about her except she dates a lot. Not that I lean out the window spying or anything. But I've noticed she'll have one boyfriend for a couple of weeks, then he'll disappear and there'll be another, then another, then another. I guess she's real choosy.'

'With those looks, she can afford to be.'

'I suppose,' Reenie grumbled. 'But she could be a little nicer to us earthlings.'

'I have an idea,' I said. 'Why don't we invite her to come join us for our barbecue on Saturday? We should try to make friends with her. After all, she is your neighbour.'

Reenie frowned at me.

'Come on, it's a nice gesture. She might even introduce

us to some of her rejects.'

We left a note in Samantha's mailbox, never expecting to see her, of course.

On Saturday at about a quarter to 12 we started the grill and put beer in the cool-box. Behind us we heard 'Yoo Hoo, it's me. Sammi.'

Reenie and I whirled round in amazement. Samantha continued talking in a slightly slurred voice, 'Oh, my good-ness those hotdogs look soo good. I could smell them from my living room and it made me soo hungry. And hamburg-ers, too. I just love hamburgers. With the works – ketchup, mustard, mayo, sliced raw onions, tomatoes. They go so good with beer. May I have one?' Not waiting for an answer, she headed straight for the cool-box.

Reenie leaned over and whispered, 'That's more than I've ever heard her say since she moved in.'

'She's sozzled,' I murmured. 'And it isn't even midday yet!'

'Well, let's join her,' Reenie laughed as we followed Sammi to the cool-box.

Almost two hours later, two beers each for us and five for Sammi, we started talking about, what else, men.

Reenie crooned the common refrain, 'Where are all the good men?' I complained about my deficiency in that department, too. Then, drying mock tears, Reenie sobbed, 'I think they're all dating Sammi.'

Samantha shocked us both when she announced, 'Yes, but they always break up with me.'

'Break up with you!' Reenie and I said in unison.

Sammi looked down. 'Well, I meet a guy, usually at a bar. We'll go out a few times but it always ends up the same.

They accuse me of being an alcoholic and don't call me any anymore.'

'Well,' Reenie ventured sympathetically, 'do you, uh, drink a lot?'

'Well, yes, because I'm no fun without a few drinks. My dates would see me like I really am – boring and shy. I don't even talk to people at work.'

Reenie and I looked at each other.

Individuals with SAD are at two to three times' greater risk of alcohol abuse and dependence on other substance abuse disorders. They frequently use alcohol to self-medicate in order to decrease anticipatory anxiety and reduce avoidance of feared social and/or performance situations.[1]

Sammi continued. 'Ever since I was a kid, I've been a loner. It wasn't because I wanted to. It's just I couldn't look anyone in the eye. In high school I didn't have any dates until I started loosening up with a few drinks. Then I'd have a great time but, if I started feeling uncomfortable, I'd just have another drink.'

Our hearts went out to Sammi.

Fifty per cent of diagnosed social phobics use alcohol to loosen themselves before attending a social event.[2]

The 50 per cent in this statistic does not mean half of all Shys. The statistic refers to *diagnosed* Shys, those who have sought professional help.

SHYBUSTER 41:
Drink and Drugs Make Shyness Worse

Drugs and alcohol can make a Shy feel more confident – but only for a very short time. It is NOT a solution to shyness. In fact, it makes it a lot worse. Not only do you run the risk of becoming dependent on your 'libation medication' or drug, but it deprives you of the satisfaction of having negotiated a social situation on your own. Not to mention hangovers.

Here is another sad statistic: *The Journal of Anxiety Disorders* published a study showing that super-shy people who drink to relieve the anguish of their shyness are far less likely to get married than the more sober Shys.[3] Sadly, that seemed like it was going to be Sammi's fate.

I've kept in touch with Reenie and she told me nothing has changed, except that Sammi looks much older than when I met her just a couple of years ago. Samantha is no longer a drop-dead gorgeous redhead. Her dates have dwindled off, and she seldom leaves the house.

" I was so shy that I could never be friendly with people at parties. I was OK with my women friends but if a man came to talk to me, I would get edgy. Especially if he gave me a compliment. I'd blush and fidget in front of him and feel so embarrassed.

But if I had a few drinks I'd feel I was cute and funny and then men didn't intimidate me so much.. So I started drinking more and enjoying that guys were paying so much attention to me.

But then one time I was at a bar with a girlfriend. I got pretty drunk and went up to these two really tough-looking guys wearing leather and chains. Anyway, the next thing I remember was waking up with a tremendous hangover and both guys in bed with me. I started to cry and one of them took me home. I realized it's better to be shy than an alcoholic, and now I'm working on my shyness in other ways. "

LINDSEY – AKRON, OHIO

how to get off the hook (half the time)

Stay Home, Guilt Free

I would never suggest this SHYBUSTER if I didn't know that anyone who starts a new programme to stop smoking/drinking/eating chocolate, etc. is bound to slip up occasionally. They'll sneak a smoke, a scotch or Snickers bar when nobody is looking. We are but poor mortals, not saints.

Of course you've tortured yourself asking, 'Shall I ... Go to the party? Ask Ms Hottie for a date? Attend the meeting? Ask Mr Fit for a lift? Join the office gang around the water-cooler?'

It's a tough choice, and rationalization is a formidable enemy. Does this sound like you?

'Should I go to that party?'

Nah, I don't like the person who is giving it.

'Shall I ask her for a date?'

It's too expensive. And we may not like each other anyway.

'Should I go chat with the gang around the water-cooler?'

Nah, they're just gossiping anyway. (Hey, maybe it's about me!)

Camouflaged Avoiding

At this stage I hope you are not *consciously* avoiding social situations. If, however, you are still tending towards 'no go' more than half the time, flip a coin. Heads I do it. Tails I don't.

That's really stupid. Why should I leave my choice to the toss of a coin?

For the same reason I love my new toothbrush. Every morning for years, as I squeezed toothpaste from the tube, my dentist's stern face haunted me in the mirror. The apparition commanded. 'Brush your teeth for a full three minutes.' But I'd always quit early, rationalizing that the extra half-minute didn't matter. Then I'd feel guilty.

Then someone gave me a toothbrush that shakes, scrubs and purrs for precisely three minutes. No more agonizing about when to quit. No more guilt pangs. My toothbrush makes the decision for me.

SHYBUSTER 42:

Toss a Coin

This one's only for Shys who avoid social situations more than half the time. Free yourself from hours of torturous thinking, vacillating and wondering whether to do something, finding a flimsy excuse, then feeling guilty. Leave the go–don't go verdict to the omnipotent coin. Your choice is made for you in two seconds. One rule: No further reflection after it's flipped. You must obey the command of the almighty coin.

Likewise, if you find yourself tending towards 'No,' leave it to the coin. Let heads or tails decide whether to go to the gathering, ask Ms Hottie for a date, attend the meeting, ask Mr Fit for a lift or join the gang round the water-cooler.

❝ There was a woman at work that I liked and we'd talked to each other once or twice but I'd never had the courage to ask her out. One week I'd think yes, but then I'd stall. Then I'd think, well, if I've stalled this long, maybe I don't want to. Then it would start all over again.

I was telling one of my buddies that I was debating whether or not to ask her out. He took a pound coin out of his pocket and said it made all the tough decisions for him. Somehow he got me to promise him that I'd ask her out if heads came up. It did. I asked her out and she seemed pleased. We're going to a movie that we both want to see. Wish me luck. ❞

KELVIN – CARDIFF, WALES

the danger of being a 'denying shy'

Confucius Said: 'A Shy Smile Is Better Than Egg on Your Face'

He didn't really, but he should have. Some Shys go to great lengths to get out of social situations and prove they are not shy, even to themselves. Many dig themselves into a hole so deep an oil drill couldn't find them.

I once met a man in Starbucks who'd come up with such a bizarre scheme for concealing his shyness to himself that it may have been catastrophic to his career.

While trying to enjoy my overpriced designer coffee, a couple of noisy kids were running around making a ruckus. I commented on it off-handedly to the young man sitting nearby. He seemed shocked that a stranger would talk to him. 'Uh, they're just normal rambunctious boys.'

'You must love children,' I said.

'Well sure, doesn't everybody?' he said, still not making any eye-contact with me.

I smiled. 'Do you have any kids?'

'No, but I'm interning as a paediatrician.' He seemed proud, in fact a tad arrogant, yet his voice was hesitant and he still made no eye-contact.

We chatted a little more. Or I should say, I chatted. He seemed to be listening, but he kept averting his eyes. I realized that he wasn't just your common-or-garden variety shy.

This poor gentleman suffered from something big-time.

I introduced myself. 'I'm Andrew,' he responded.

Suspecting a bad case of the shys and seeing no ring on Andrew's finger, I purposefully brought the subject round to dating and other social situations.

A painful expression flooded his face. 'All the women I meet want just one thing, to marry a doctor. So I gave up on them long ago. Besides, parties are a waste of time.'

'Do you attend many?' I hesitantly asked.

'As few as possible!' he shot back. He told me the hospital where he interned held many social functions and the doctors and interns brought their wives or significant others.

It was obvious that this chap didn't have even an *in*significant other due to his views on dating.

'The parties are horrible. All anyone does is make stupid small-talk, and I'm no good at talking small.' I began to realize that Andrew didn't consciously realize he was shy. Therapists call this type of person a 'Socially Avoidant Personality'.

" I HATE parties. Detest them. Being besieged by dozens of people drunk out of their gourds and making superficial conversation with other phonies they couldn't care less about. And a bunch of guys just wanting to jump the women's bones. That is certainly not my idea of a good time. I avoid them like the plague. And feel free to use my name."

RICHARD – HOUSTON, TEXAS

Richard should ask himself if he might be a 'closet shy', one of the many people who won't admit their shyness to themselves. They find other rationalizations for avoiding intimidating situations.

In another part of his message, Richard wrote,

> **"I am very lonely and am looking for a meaningful relationship with a woman. But I haven't met 'the one' yet."**
>
> RICHARD – HOUSTON, TEXAS

I asked Andrew, 'Have you been to any of the parties recently?'

He rolled his eyes. 'Yes, and it was a disaster.'

I gently ventured, 'What happened?'

'I figured if I took a sociable lady, she'd do the small-talk for me. Then I wouldn't have to make foolish banter.'

'So whom did you take?'

He answered sarcastically, 'A lady'. I was silent, hoping he would continue. 'I occasionally go to a "gentlemen's club". There's a topless dancer there who took a shine to me. Marla. She said I was different from the average guy who frequents the club.

'Anyway, the American Board of Pediatrics sponsored a must-attend function. Since Marla was the only woman I knew, and she was congenial, I figured she'd be the ideal candidate. Marla said she'd meet me at the party.'

Unfortunately, though predictably, Andrew's story does not have a happy ending. Marla arrived at the reception showing more cleavage than a Vegas showgirl, and wearing trousers so tight it looked like she'd been sewn into them.

'Marla did indeed converse with the other guests,' Andrew said wryly, 'but when she opened her mouth, it was evident that she was not in the postdoctoral training programme. At one point, she started telling everybody where we'd met and all about her job. Everybody was laughing. I know what they were thinking of me.

'If I have to go to parties like that all the time, I'm not sure the medical profession is for me.'

> **Some shy subjects set up 'guaranteed failure' situations, both professionally and personally. That way they can avoid situations they are uncomfortable with – and blame it on something or somebody else.[1]**

By the way, and talking of exotic dancers, I don't mean to denigrate anyone who works for hard-earned money in an honest profession. In fact, topless dancers have been able to accomplish something professionally that many Shys have not. And that is to find a job which fully utilizes their God-given (or augmented) talents.

It wasn't my place to counsel Andrew, but obviously he had set up a situation where he didn't have to blame, or even recognize, his own shyness. How convenient! He could accuse Marla and be psychologically off the hook for future social events.

SHYBUSTER 43:

Bring a Note from Your Subconscious

Just like little Jimmy needs Mum's note to prove he's not been bunking off school, you need confirmation from your subconscious that there's another reason you can't attend the gathering. Little Jimmy's 'I hate school' won't cut it. And neither does your 'I hate parties.' Before turning down any social situation, make sure there is a reason and it's not that you're a 'Socially Avoidant Personality' – or SAP (my acronym, sorry, but if the shoe fits …)

As for Andrew, he has at least chosen to enter a field that accommodates his shy personality. He loves kids and feels no shyness around them. He knows he is helping them and, as a paediatrician, he will have more contact with kids than grown-ups. I hope it works out for him. Of course, he is limiting the social side of himself, and it doesn't sound like he'll ever meet a woman he can settle down with, but if a Shy isn't ready to acknowledge their shyness or motivated to do something about it, like you have done by reading this book, then there's not a lot of help that can be offered them.

section IX
fearless conversation

terrified
of being trite?

Be a 'You Firstie'

The home side in football has the advantage. The card-counter in blackjack has the advantage. And the person who starts conversation in chance meetings has the advantage.

Pushy people do it too much. Sures do it half the time. Shys hardly ever speak first.

Your mind is racing. *Will I say something foolish? I can't just say something like, 'How are you?' because it's too trite. If I start a conversation, I'll have to make more small-talk. Gosh, I guess I better not say anything.*

Here's a novel idea. Why not just say, 'Hi! How are you?' Of course it's banal, but it is the accepted form of greeting in our country. Naturally, nobody expects a real answer. They don't want to hear you have a hernia or haemorrhoids. They just want an 'I'm fine.' But let's go a step further with that one.

'I'm Fine' Isn't Enough

Now is the time to flaunt your friendly feathers. Instead of ending the exchange with a trite 'Fine,' extend the human interaction by saying something about your day. Of course they couldn't care less about the particulars. It's simply the overture to a relationship.

Of course it's a cliché, but even talking about the weather is OK. Eavesdrop on *anyone* and you'll find that's precisely what most conversational openings are, all over the world.

Not to worry. After any inauspicious opening, something lovely happens. The more small-talk two people make, the more apt it is to evolve into interesting communicating.

SHYBUSTER 44:
Be Banal, But Not Brief

When they ask, 'How are you?' it's not fine just to say 'I'm fine.' That aborts conversation before it ever takes off. Extend it by adding a simple sentence or two, and they'll immediately put you on their 'confident and friendly colleagues' list.

It doesn't even matter if the news of your day is mundane. Just deliver it in an upbeat I'm-thrilled-to-tell-you voice. An example: After their perennial 'How are you?' you could say, 'Good. But I've been all over town looking for a new briefcase, and I hate to shop. Don't you?'

Perhaps he tells you his brother-in-law just gave him a briefcase. Yawn. But smile and respond like that is electrifying news. Ask him where his brother-in-law lives. Pretend you're fascinated that he's from Barnsley. Ask what Barnsley

---

SHYBUSTER 45:

Sound Dazzled Over the Dullest Things

No matter how boring your words, say them in a
'This is the greatest thing since Velcro' tone. And
guess what? They will sound interesting to your
listener.

---

is like. (Now you're playing a good hand of small-talk, the
game that many Shys fear most.)

Using *Their* Name Says Something about *You*

In spite of the millions of times they've heard it, hearing
their name roll off your tongue makes them feel as warm
and fuzzy as a kitten. But did you know it also says a lot
about you? Subliminally they hear, 'I am confident,' 'I like
you,' 'I respect you,' and 'We are friends.'

Understandably, as with mastering any new skill, it's difficult to gauge how much to use the other person's name.
Soon you'll get the feel of when it's appropriate. For now,
lay it on them at the greeting and the parting. 'Good morning [Name].' 'Good to see you, [Name].' 'So long, [Name].'
'Nice talking with you, [Name].'

Be careful, though. If you use their name too much, you
could come across as insincere and condescending. Not to
mention annoying.

I had a problem with my computer several months ago. I called tech support to report that every time I tried to open a file, I'd get an error message. The conversation went something like this:

Techie: OK. What's your name?

Me: Leil

Techie: Are you sitting in front of your computer now, Leil?

Me: Yes I am.

Techie: Good, Leil. Now double-click on 'My Computer'

Me: OK, I've done that.

Techie: Leil, now I want you to click on 'Folders'. Have you done that, Leil?

Me: Yes.

Techie: Now, Leil, scroll down to the Directory the file is in.

Me: OK (I wanted to shout, 'ALL RIGHT, ALREADY, I KNOW WHAT MY *$@ NAME IS!)

Techie: OK, Leil, now I want you to double-click on the file that you can't open.

At this point I wanted to double-click on his head with a hammer.

SHYBUSTER 46:

Use Their Moniker in Moderation

Say someone's name in greeting and parting. It makes them feel all warm and fuzzy. But if you use it too much, it comes across as a nervous habit and makes that someone feel as warm and fuzzy as steel wool.

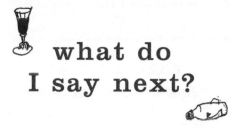

what do I say next?

Better Than Their Humanoid Sounds

With this SHYBUSTER you won't need to anguish about what to say next. Most people, while *supposedly* listening to someone talk, make various humanoid sounds: 'Hmm,' 'Uh huh,' 'OK,' 'Yeah.' Unfortunately Shys have a difficult time making these comforting noises because their 'me' thoughts get in the way.

So, Shys, instead of being a run-of-the-mill hummer, have some 'keep talking' questions at the ready. The familiar 'How?' 'Where?' 'What?' 'Who?' and 'When?' questions work wonders to keep the other person talking when a pause occurs. You might ask:

'What did he say then?'

'Where else did you visit?'

'How did you accomplish that?'

It's a win-win situation. The other person will love the sound of their own patter, keep talking more, and you won't suffer from 'What do I say next?' syndrome.

Recently I was gabbing away at someone and realized the poor guy hadn't said a word. I paused to give him a chance. He just said, 'Go on, Leil. Tell me more.'

I didn't need a second invitation. I dived into another 20-minute monologue and came away thinking what a great conversationalist *he* was.

SHYBUSTER 47:
Ask 'Go On' Questions

Leave 'Uh huh' and 'OK' to the robot crowd. Be ready with a few 'encourager' questions. He or she will be thrilled that you want to hear more – and you won't need to come up with convivial and clever conversation.

" One thing that helped me get over my fear of making small-talk with strangers is realizing that they don't really care about your opinion. So why even try to interject your views? I learned that it was a piece of cake to keep them going with an occasional question about what they were saying. "

RALPH – GREENVILLE, KENTUCKY

the proven
eye-contact cure

Dr Daffy Did It

A fabulous friendship with a fellow flight attendant began on an overseas flight. We had just finished serving dinner to 200 passengers and, back in the galley, wiping roast beef off our uniforms, she sensitively asked me why I didn't make much eye-contact with the passengers. I liked her gentle approach and told her I was shy. We talked a lot that flight, and by the time the sun was streaming in the windows, we knew we'd be good friends.

Daphne (Daffy for short) shared a flat with her brother in Astoria, New York City, a neighbourhood known as 'Little Greece'. While visiting her once between flights, she said, 'Leil, I think I have a cure for your problem with eye-contact.'

'Oh good.' *Here comes another flop,* I thought. 'Really? Tell me.'

'I want you to look directly into my eyes, and I'll look into yours. We'll see how long we can hold it.'

'What?'

'Do it!'

I broke up laughing each time.

'Leil, stop it. I'm deadly serious about this.' She stood up in exasperation. 'Go ahead and enjoy being shy for the rest of your life. See if I care.'

That convinced me. Later, after half-a-dozen feeble

attempts, I was able to look directly into her eyes for about 30 seconds and feel at ease.

'Wow, how did you learn that, Daffy?'

'At university we were studying how important eye-contact is. One afternoon the professor asked us all to sit next to somebody we didn't know and stare into their eyes. Most of us cracked up. But all week he made us change partners and stare longer and longer until we could do it for a full minute. Then he asked us to carry on a conversation with each other and not break eye-contact even for a second.

'Leil, the results were unbelievable. When we discussed it Monday morning, everyone reported they'd made more eye-contact than ever before with everybody they'd talked to over the weekend.'

In the Netherlands, VVM, the Association of Shy People founded in 1988, has been extremely effective with people who are profoundly shy. During their training all members must look someone in the eyes for graduated amounts of time. These exercises have been found to also help problems with blushing and not taking initiative.[1]

'Yeah, but you're a friend, Daf. I don't think I could do it with a stranger.'

She smiled. 'Let's see.' Her brother Nicias, whom I had never met, was upstairs studying. Daffy called him from the staircase, 'Nicky, could you come down and help us with something?'

When I looked up to say 'Hello,' my heart leapt up to my throat. Nicias was nothing short of a Greek God. Daffy explained what we had been doing and asked him to take her place in the 'eye-contact game'. It would have been difficult enough to gaze into the eyes of a 'normal' person, but with Adonis! For Shys, the more desirable someone is, the harder it is to look at them.

> **❝ I worked at a grocery store as a teenager and developed a crush on a young factory worker who came in on his breaks. I couldn't talk to him or make eye-contact even if my life depended on it. My face would blush if he even talked to me, but I always looked forward to his visits. ❞**
>
> DEEANA – CLAREMONT, NEW HAMPSHIRE

'Daffy, I can't ...'

'Yes you can, Leil.'

When she said 'Go!' our eyes locked. Blush spread over my face like wildfire, and my heart felt like a jack-hammer. Slowly, very slowly, the fire simmered down and the jack-hammer switched into low gear.

When Daffy gauged my vital signs were returning to normal, she said, 'OK, time's up.' Nicias went back up to study. I threw my arm up to my forehead and feigned a faint. 'I cannot believe what I just did, Daffy.'

SHYBUSTER 48:
The Eyeball Lock

Assure a close friend or relative that you haven't gone bonkers, then ask for their help with the staring exercise. When you've worked your way up to a minute, have a conversation with them while maintaining exaggerated eye-contact.

I promise that the next time you are speaking with a stranger, it won't feel like you are looking a charging bull in the eyes.

It's tough, and if you don't succeed the first time, try again. And again. And again. While conversing, of course, your eyes should take fleeting breaks from theirs.

What you consider exaggerated eye-contact will soon become natural. Don't expect immediate success with this one. Direct eye-contact for a Shy is like staring down the barrel of a gun. But keep at it.

Eye-contact Is Smart and Sexy, Too

Researchers conducted a test to see if there were a correlation between eye-contact and intelligence. There was. The subjects who scored higher on the IQ tests maintained more eye-contact while conversing than the other subjects.[2]

SHYBUSTER 49:
Looking Longer Looks Smart

Extended eye-contact with the person you are speaking with gives the impression of being capable of comfortably processing your thoughts while talking, and not being distracted by their eye-contact.

You probably already know that intense eye-contact between a man and a woman, gives love and lust a big boost. A study called 'The Effects of Mutual Gaze on Feelings of Romantic Love' confirmed it.[3] Look deeply into a special someone's eyes and you'll feel the 'chemistry' at work.

SHYBUSTER 50:
Lingering Looks Kindle 'Chemistry'

If you don't want that fire to go out when your eyes meet, do not look away. The longer you gaze into his or her eyes, the more potential there is for sparks to ignite.

" My shyness was much worse with men that I was interested in dating. I had a crush on a guy at my gym. I know he liked me because I'd catch him looking at me when I was working out. One time I looked straight at him, too. He smiled and I almost fainted. I even went to a bookstore to read up on how to flirt or talk to him. I did my research and picked the day to make conversation. When the day came, I choked. I just could not get past my crippling shyness, I was terrified. I was so frustrated and upset at my inability to even look at him that I didn't go back for a week. "

RENEE – MONTPELIER, VERMONT

chameleons
should choose their
colours carefully

Personality Is 'Catching'

It's fiction that those cute micro-dinosaurs called Chameleons change colour to match their surroundings. But it's fact that people change to match theirs. If you find a confident friend who has an outgoing personality, just by being around them yours becomes more outgoing, too. If your good buddy talks to strangers, you start yapping it up with new people, too. If your cool friend goes to parties and has a good time, you find yourself tagging along. It's a simple case of monkey see, monkey do. (No insult intended.) Daffy was an invaluable friend and I was a grateful monkey trying to be as outgoing as she was.

Singles are usually looking for love, and marrieds want to spice up their relationship. Everyone, however, should take the time to find a good same-sex friend.[1]

" There is a very outgoing girl who works in the same office as me. We became friends and one night she dragged me out to a club that had dancing until 2 a.m. I wanted to leave but she was my ride home. Fortunately it was dark in the corners so I hid out there and watched everybody else dancing in the centre of the room.

My friend, whose name was Rachael, was actually walking up to guys and talking to them, and then they would dance. I always wanted to be like her but I was too shy.

She found me sitting in the corner and scolded me. I explained to her for the umpteenth time that I was shy. I don't know whether she'd had a drink or what but she seriously told me that she wasn't going to give me a ride home unless I went up to some guy and asked him to dance. I couldn't do that but I did manage to go talk to one. After that, I felt a little better and talked to several more. They seemed happy that I'd walked over to them.

DANIELLE – GREENWICH, CONNECTICUT

I'd wager that the next time Danielle goes to the disco with Rachael, she won't hide out in a dark corner. Wanting to be like a supportive and confident friend gives a big boost to your Stamping Out Shyness (SOS) campaign. If Rachael had been shy, too, they would have sat together in the corner all evening being miserable.

SHYBUSTER 51:
A Little Shove from a Non-Shy Friend

It may not be conscious copy-catting, but, like chameleons, we take on the colouration of those we hang with. Find a non-shy friend. Tell them you'd welcome their nudging you into new situations.

Note to parents: Encourage your child to have a good friend. A study called 'Shyness and Friendship Quality' has found that:

Having at least one high-quality friendship before the age of 10 was associated with a greater sense of classmate support, decreased anxiety and improved self-worth, even among shy [children].[2]

become an expert
– on anything!

'How Can You Tell a Poisonous One from a Good One?'

I attended a faculty picnic after a college speech I'd given a few years a go. I sat with the faculty on the campus afterward chatting and scarfing down hamburgers. While talking with one of the teachers I commented on a 40-something-looking man who had been sitting alone all afternoon.

'Oh, that's Professor Wagner,' came the reply, 'the head of the biology department. He's a very kind man. But he's shy and hardly talks to anyone. The only time he's comfortable is when he's in front of a class or talking about his field.' Then the teacher laughed, 'Don't get him talking about mushrooms or he'll talk your ear off!'

I crossed the green to introduce myself and, from his demeanour, I could tell he was a Highly Sensitive Shy.

'Ms Turner tells me you teach a course on mushrooms.'

'Uh, yes,' he said haltingly.

'I've always been interested in mushrooms,' I lied. 'Can you tell me a little about your class?'

He started slowly, but then the plug popped out of the dam. He started gushing about matsutakes, chanterelles, boletes and a dozen names that I assume were mushrooms. My only contribution to his monologue was 'How can you tell a poisonous one from a good one?'

That made it stunningly obvious that mushrooms weren't exactly my thing. He smiled and slithered back into his shy shell.

Excuse Me for Taking Up Space on Your Planet

After a rather lengthy moment of silence, he said, 'You'll have to excuse me, I'm very shy.' He then gave me one of the Shy's typical 'Excuse me for taking up space on your planet' looks.

I told him I was writing about the subject, and asked if I could talk with him for a few minutes. He cautiously conceded but gave monosyllabic answers to most of my questions.

I guided the conversation to his private life. He told me that, although he was 42, he would like to marry and maybe start a family, but he was too shy to ask any women for a date.

'Mind, I don't meet any women. Besides,' he added, 'it's too late for me to think about getting married. All the other professors already have children or teenagers.'

'Professor Wagner,' I asked, 'are there any mushroom clubs? I mean mushroom societies? I mean associations? Well, groups of people of people who love mushrooms? Biologically, I mean. Not just eating them?'

Understandably, he looked confused. 'Uh, I think so. But I don't think I'd learn anything because, well, I probably know at least as much as they do about mushrooms.'

He hadn't got the point. 'Professor Wagner, may I make a suggestion?' He nodded. 'I think you might enjoy going to a meeting of people who are interested in mushrooms.

They would be very grateful if you shared your know-ledge. You would be giving information instead of receiving. I strongly suggest it.'

Just then, it started to drizzle, a sure sign that the picnic was over and it was time to say our goodbyes.

Several years passed and the college invited me to speak again. I asked the event co-ordinator how Professor Wagner was doing and told her I'd like to say hello.

'Let me get his number for you.' She looked at her faculty list. 'I'm sure it will be OK if you call him at home.'

Even a Mushroom Can Sprout Love

I dialled his number and a woman answered. Her voice was sweet but barely audible. I asked to speak to Professor Wagner. The next thing I heard was a soft, 'Mike, honey, it's for you.'

He seemed pleased I'd called. Without sounding like I was trying to probe, I said, 'The woman who answered has a lovely voice. Is she a relation?'

'Yes, she's my wife. And she is wonderful. Oh, I'm so sorry, I should have called you. After we spoke a few years ago, I thought about what you said and found a local league of mushroom-lovers, and I met Sandra there. It was a long time before either of us had the courage to approach each other. She's very shy, but one time on a mushroom-gathering trip we started walking together. We have so much in common. One thing led to another, and ...'

Both Professor Wagner and Sandra had been passionate about mushrooms. Happily they now have each other to be passionate about, too.

SHYBUSTER 52:

Find Others Who Share Your Passion

Type the name of your hobby into your search
engine. Narrow the million hits with the word 'club',
'league', 'organization' or 'association'. Then shave
it down more with the name of your area. Chances
are you'll come up with a nearby group of people
who are passionate about the same thing.

Bernardo Carducci, one of the world's top shyness
researchers, has written that shy people may need to take an
especially active role in finding groups of like-minded people.

The Internet is a godsend for finding groups of people
who share the same interests.

how to answer the inevitable question

Your Enthralling Answer to a Cliché Query

It's a sure bet. Within five minutes of meeting someone they'll ask, 'What do you do?' Don't flounder for the right words every time. Rehearse a concise upbeat job description to make it sound like you have the most exciting work in the world.

Sadly, many Shys, when asked the inevitable, drop their eyes and say, 'Oh, I'm just a ...' Once I was visiting a company and got lost in a corridor. I asked an attractive woman where someone's office was. She lead me to my destination. I thanked her and said, 'By the way, what department are you in?'

'Oh, I'm just the receptionist,' she answered.

I wanted to shake her for seeing her job as unimportant. 'No, you are not just the receptionist. You are THE receptionist.' She looked at me as though I were a little strange.

SHYBUSTER 53:
Rehearse Your Mini-CV

Don't just answer the inevitable, 'What do you do?'
with the name of your job. Plan a *proud* response.
Speaking negatively of your job is just another way
of saying 'I'm a loser and unable to achieve what I
want in life.' Rehearse your upbeat mini-monologue
in the mirror and deliver it enthusiastically as
though you're so happy to have been asked this
novel question.

nobody expects you to perform

Some of the Best Conversationalists Never Open Their Mouths

The first call I made when returning from the first flight after my eye-contact lesson was to thank Daffy.

'Daf, I cannot tell you how easy it was to look at all my passengers – bingo, right in the eyes.' As I was blithering on, she got that 'I've-got-something-up-my-sleeve' sound in her voice.

'Can you come over in about an hour?' she asked.

'Well, sure, but ...' She'd rung off.

When I arrived, Daffy notified me, 'Today you're taking your next step towards getting your "doctorate in eye-contact".' I could see she was enjoying playing her new role as my therapist.

'Oh no, what now?'

'My mother is giving a small luncheon party today and ...' Terror filled my face. 'Don't worry, it won't be so bad.'

She briefed me. 'This time, in addition to eye-contact, I want you to listen carefully to whomever is speaking, and smile and nod when appropriate.'

'But I can't make small-talk with strangers just like that.'

'Here's the beauty of it, Leil. You won't have to. My mom volunteers for an organization which orients new immigrants. Today is a welcome lunch for 14 of them and I don't think one speaks English. So, don't you see? The pressure is off. You don't have to say a word. Just smile, act friendly and look them in the eyes.'

We arrived at a loud Greek taverna and it seemed like everyone was talking simultaneously in a language which was, well, Greek to me.

Daphne's mother was sitting at a large table with the new arrivals. Daffy gave her a kiss on the cheek and introduced me. Her mother suggested I sit near her since I didn't speak any Greek.

Daffy winked. 'Absolutely not. I'm putting Leil right over there between those two men.' When she introduced me, I smiled at them weakly. They smiled at me broadly. From what I could gather their names were Leonidas and Scopas.

'Don't worry,' Daffy said, 'I've told them you don't speak Greek. I'm going over to sit with Mom now.'

'Daf, don't leave me.' She was gone.

Greek to Me

The waiter put a strange dish in front of me which looked like octopus vinaigrette. I could tell that Leonidas was asking me if I liked it. I managed to swallow the slimy thing, nodding my head dramatically. I even clapped my hands softly to show I loved it.

I couldn't believe how relaxed I was getting. For the first time sitting at a table with a group of strangers, I didn't want to be invisible. In fact I sat up tall, pushed my hair back, and even smiled at one of the good-looking Greek guys at the other end of the table.

Then it got hairy. The Greek hottie excused himself from his dinner partners and headed straight towards me. I panicked. *What if he speaks English? What if I have to talk to him?*

He bowed graciously and introduced himself in Greek. Daffy raced to the rescue. He spoke briefly to her and Daffy beamed at me. 'Leil, Tylissus wants to ask you for a date.'

'Who wants to do what?'

'He's serious.'

'You've got to be kidding, Daf. Tell him that's very nice of him. I'm flattered. But, Daf, tell him I'm married. Tell him I have I communicable disease. Tell him I'm a lesbian.'

On the way back to Daffy's place, I announced that I didn't feel at all uneasy at the party.

'Sure, why not?' she said. 'Nobody expected you to say anything.' That whacked me like a killer wave. She was right! It was because *I didn't have to perform*. Nobody was expecting me to speak. Nobody was going to judge me by what I said.

Nobody Expects You to Talk

Shys, it would be the same for you if your luncheon companions didn't speak English. You wouldn't fear you'd say something stupid or inappropriate. If they were strangers you knew you wouldn't see again, you wouldn't be that anxious or timid.

Well, guess what? Even when everybody in a group is speaking crystal-clear English, and some of them know you, you are not expected to perform. You don't have to say anything if you don't want to – all you have to do is listen, smile and nod. These flag your friendliness. The more nods and smiles you bestow on another person, the more personality they'll think you have. The fact that a warm receptive listener doesn't say a word is hardly noticeable.

SHYBUSTER 54:
Look, Nod, Smile

Don't fret if you're not yet prepared to speak up in a group. Just give them the never-fails formula. Look them in the eyes, smile and nod when appropriate. I promise you, you will be a very welcome addition to the group because everyone loves a good listener. You will be perceived as Mr or Ms Congeniality. And you don't need to say a word until you're ready.

I have a good friend called Nate. Nate doesn't talk much. But whenever I tell him *anything* he gives me an enormous grin and says 'Really?' or 'That's great' (as though my lame comment really were). It's such a pleasure being around Nate. Apparently a beautiful and brilliant attorney, Deborah, thought so too. They just got married.

I once asked Deborah how they'd met. She told me Nate was one of her clients. 'I'd never met such a good listener. He's so much fun,' she told me. 'And he has that big smile.'

passion slays shyness

Passion Makes You Forget Being Shy

I discovered the remedial effect passion has on shyness when I was 12. Two boys, Donny and Bobby Baker, lived next door. They always teased me, so whenever they played outside I'd run into the house.

Doing my homework on the porch one Saturday afternoon, I heard boisterous laughter in their back garden. I scooped up my books to go inside. Just then I heard an animal's piercing screech. I spun around.

There was Bobby, gleefully swinging a stray cat by the tail while his little brother sprayed it with a garden hose. Not for a split second did shyness enter my consciousness. I dropped my books and shrieked at them like hawk out for blood.

They laughed and held the tortured creature up for me to get a better view. That did it. Full of fury, I dashed down the porch stairs, snatched a shovel by the garage door, raised it over my head and took off after them.

Flabbergasted, they dropped the cat and ran. The cat scurried away, hopefully back to its family to be licked back to health. It wasn't until I reached my porch that I saw the menacing weapon in my hands. I stared at it in disbelief. My passion for animals had momentarily overcome my shyness.

> **"** Getting really involved in something I loved
> doing helped me get rid of my shyness.
> Years ago, I started DJ-ing at parties. I'd get
> so involved in the music that it was easy to
> talk to women that I would normally be
> afraid to speak to. They even came up to me
> for requests. That helped me to feel more
> comfortable about myself. **"**

BUDDY – LOS ANGELES, CALIFORNIA

Turn Off the 'ME' Show

Books often suggest going to seminars as a good anti-shyness strategy. You should offer to hand out programmes, take tickets, etc. It's good advice. In fact, very good advice. However, if your main purpose for being there is to practise mingling, you're still watching the 'ME' Show. Thinking back, if I had been at a 'People for Persecuted Animals' meeting I would have been fixated on victimized animals, not myself.

When you are totally passionate about something, you forget yourself because you're so absorbed in your purpose.

> **"** I am 48 and, when I divorced 11 years ago,
> I found it impossible to get back onto the
> dating scene. I was too shy to go to parties
> or even think of approaching a man. I have
> always loved wine, though, and consider
> myself something of a connoisseur. Just

recently I've started going to wine-tastings and have met several very nice men. It's so easy to talk to them because they love wine too and we have something to talk about.**"**

DIANA – MELBOURNE, AUSTRALIA

What about you? What is your passion? Is it the environment? World hunger? Health care? If you are passionate about where you live, help your community stop those greedy, insensitive moguls from defacing the landscape with another shopping mall. Find your passion and go for it. SHY-BUSTER 18 will help you to locate your purpose and your passion.

SHYBUSTER 55:
Stamp Out Shyness with Your Particular Passion

When you join a cause you feel passionate about, you're not thinking 'What do they think of me?' You are concentrating on 'What can all of us do to further this cause?' When the goal is foremost in your mind, shyness fades into the background.

Additional benefit: A bond grows between people working for the same cause, and quality friendships form automatically.

The Incredible Power of Passion

The power of passion is so mighty that, even after you become a certified Sure, it will help you achieve other personal goals. It did for me.

I once had a little company called 'Showtime at Sea'. My partner, a wonderful gay man named Chip, and I produced entertainment for cruise ships. We had travelled the world together and he was my closest and dearest friend.

Chip contracted HIV and I nursed him throughout a horrible and painful illness until the time of his death. At his funeral, his sister asked if anyone wanted to say a few words. Three or four relatives stood and spoke of Chip's kindness and other good qualities, but I realized they knew nothing of his professional accomplishments. To them, he was just Jan and Nick's little boy, grown up.

I found myself unable to stay seated. My hand shot up and I almost ran to the podium at the front of the funeral hall. I spoke passionately and unselfconsciously for 20 minutes about what a talented, loving and brilliant man Chip was. Not for one moment did I feel like I was giving a speech to a group. The mission was to inform his extended family about Chip's very special gifts.

Of course I didn't think about it at the time, but that experience was a step in 'graduated exposure' that contributed to my becoming a professional speaker who speaks to groups of sometimes 10,000 people. But it's only when I lose myself in the passion of what I'm saying that I feel no insecurity.

Shys, if you must give presentations to people, volunteer to speak at a church or community event first. When I decided I wanted to be a professional speaker, I spoke for the

Chamber of Commerce, the Rotary Club, and any other roomful of ears that would have me.

section X

sure-fire extinguishers for shyness

a dare a day
drives shyness
away

It's Better to Be Me

It's time to throw away your mask, real or imagined, and conquer your challenges as yourself.

First step: List the situations which make your hands sweat and your heart quake. Then do a mental 'sort' – simplest to scariest, of course.

Incidentally, you might be interested in how your hotspots compare to those of other Shys. Researchers polled Shys about which situations they found most intimidating.[1] The three most menacing were:

1. meeting and talking with strangers (70%)
2. meeting and talking with members of the opposite sex (64%)
3. meeting and talking with authority figures (48%)

When you've finished your inventory of ordeals, take out your date book. Assign yourself one challenge a day for each day of the week. Naturally take into consideration what activities are feasible on which days of the week. Try explaining to your employer that you spent yesterday at the spa because having massages makes you nervous! Save that for your Saturday dare.

This week, your list might look something like this:

Sunday: Take a walk in the park and smile at people.

Next Sunday: Smile at an attractive stranger – or two or three or more – in the park.

Third Sunday ...

Monday: Ask three strangers on the street 'Excuse me, could you tell me what time it is?'

Next Monday: Compliment three strangers (in a grocery store or in the queue for the cashpoint, etc.) on something they are wearing, their cute kid, whatever.

Third Monday ...

Tuesday: Talk to someone you know while taking the lift.

Next Tuesday: Talk to a stranger or superior while taking the lift.

Third Tuesday ...

Wednesday: Join a casual office conversation.

Next Wednesday: Ask one of your office colleagues to join you for lunch.

Third Wednesday ...

Thursday: Speak up during the morning meeting.

Next Thursday: Bring up a new subject in the morning meeting.

Third Thursday ...

Friday: Chat to someone of the opposite sex, not necessarily someone you are attracted to.

Next Friday: Ask that other-gendered person to join you for some social activity. (Women, it's the 21st century, you can do this too.)

Third Friday ...

Saturday: Go shopping, talk to a dozen salespeople, and buy something returnable.

Next Saturday: Return that something and ask for a refund.

Third Saturday ...

Keep kicking it up a notch each succeeding week. Jot down how you feel after each challenge.

Troubleshooting: If you're not satisfied with your performance, take another shot at it.

SHYBUSTER 56:

Do Your Daily Dare

Set up your Dare-a-Day programme at the beginning of the week. That way you'll know that when you get to work next Monday you'll be that much more confident than you were the week before.

Extra hint: It's human nature to find a reason not to do something. Make it more difficult to weasel out of your Dare-a-Day programme by telling a friend or family member what you're up to, and reporting back to them daily. Let them be the judge of whether your excuses hold water or not.

You've Got to Be Kidding! Are You Nuts?

Now it's time for a big leap. Get some practice hearing sarcasm or scorn aimed at you so you can learn to take it in your stride. How?

Get funky. Do something way out there – anonymously and by phone, of course.

Example: Call a men's clothing store to ask if they carry trousers with an 88-inch waist and 19-inch inseam. Then deal with their 'What? You've got to be kidding!' reaction.

Call a florist's in July and give them a hard time because they don't carry mistletoe. Deal with their 'What? You've got to be kidding!' reaction.

Call a restaurant and ask them to read you the whole menu with the prices. Deal with their 'What? You've got to be kidding!' reaction.

When you get that reaction, don't back down. Stick to your guns and play along with it for a while.

And, by the way, I understand your hesitance about invading someone's day. But think of it this way: You're not really hassling them. They'll have great fun telling their colleagues 'You won't believe the mad call I got today!'

make shopping
a valuable part
of SOS

> **❝** I hate shopping because I'm always
> embarrassed to tell the salesperson I'm just
> looking. I feel so guilty if they show me a
> few things and I leave not buying even one.
> I buy a lot of things by mail-order but I don't
> like it because a lot of things don't fit and I
> have to send them back. But at least the
> mail-order people don't know me. **❞**
>
> PAMELA – TULSA, OKLAHOMA

Shopping and interacting with salespeople is a super way to
practise your social skills. They're all standing there just
waiting to interact with you. Go for it. Make everything you
buy part of your Stamping Out Shyness programme.

SHYBUSTER 57:
Inspect Six, Buy One

Even when you know you're going to choose a specific item in a store, *always* ask to be shown five others first. It's fabulous social-skills practice, and you still please the salesperson with a purchase.

a little help from man's best friend

A New Twist on Trite Advice

Of course chatting with strangers is an excellent confidence-builder. But wouldn't it be great if you didn't have to make the first move? And wouldn't it be even more lovely if admiring passers-by approached *you* with a smile, a compliment and an easy-to-answer question?

I'm sure you've been deluged with advice and, no doubt, 'Get a Dog' is top of the list. But here is where we surpass that hackneyed recommendation. Choose a canine that has an unusual and engrossing history. That way, when people stop you on the street, as they inevitably will, you can regale them with stories of your 'best friend's' history and heritage, a subject you'll soon be expert at.

Get a Look-alike Dog

Even better, get a dog that matches your appearance or your personality. What?

Seriously, there is inexplicable charm to the combo of you and your look-alike (sort of) pooch. I'll never forget a striking woman I once saw walking an Afghan Hound down Fifth Avenue in New York City. Both her and her dog's cashmere-coloured hair was waving in the wind. (It didn't hurt that Afghan Hounds have widely spaced hip joints which makes their derrieres swing like a model sashaying down the catwalk.)

Men, of course you'll want a 'tough and manly' dog. Obviously forget French Poodles or other puny pooches. Depending on your appearance, go with a Dalmatian or Doberman Pincher. If you're short, you can't go wrong with a Bulldog. As masculine though it may be, however, avoid the Pit Bull. It will have the opposite effect, making strangers keep a wide berth.

Women, naturally you want a stylish bitch. Try to have your canine's hair colour be similar to yours. People can't help but admire the similar shade of your tresses.

Unless you will be ostracized by your family, go for a bizarre breed, the stranger-looking the better. Of course, some bizarre breeds cost a lot. There are a lot of fabulous funny-looking mutts at the pound. You'll be doing the canine world a favour by choosing one that nobody else in their right mind would want.

Of course, a dog isn't just for Christmas, nor for instigating conversations. But if you're thinking about getting a pet, then a conversation-starting dog might be just the ticket to help you overcome some of your shyness around strangers!

SHYBUSTER 58:
Attention-getter on a Leash

Prepare yourself with some engrossing small-talk about your pooch. Then leave it to the admiring strangers to make the approach for your conversation practice.

" I was using the cashpoint one night when an attractive woman walked by with a big dog. I smiled at her. I finished up with the cashpoint and she started with it. While she was using it, I started petting her dog and picked up the lead that she had dropped.

The woman said to me, 'Are you stealing my dog?' She said it in a kind of cutesy, possibly flirtatious way. Unfortunately, I didn't take the bait. I was so shy that I simply said 'No' and handed her the lead. I thought she thought I really was stealing her dog.

Of course, later I thought I should have said 'Yes!' She clearly liked me. But in the moment I just didn't have the nerve to say anything else. "

RON – BURLINGTON, KENTUCKY

social blooper remedy

The Chicken Little Syndrome

Shys forever fear they'll do the wrong thing, at the wrong time, in the wrong way.[1]

Ms Shy is lunching with office colleagues at a restaurant to welcome several new employees. She hesitates at the doorway. *Should I shake hands with them? Where should I sit if no one indicates my chair? Where should I put my purse?* More imagined calamities: *What if I spill my water and everyone looks at me? What if I mispronounce somebody's name? What if I sit in the wrong place?* What if ... ? What if ...? What if ...? Some Shys sound just like Chicken Little, who insisted that the sky was falling.

Great News

You probably know precisely what to do in most social situations. In one study, researchers asked Shys how they would handle a variety of difficult social circumstances.[2] Shys even surprised the researchers with their cool, calm and correct answers.

The Shy who wondered if she should shake hands answered, 'Well, I suppose I'd look around to see if other new arrivals were shaking hands.' *Right!*

Researcher: 'What if you should spill your water?'

Mr Shy: 'I guess I'd mop it up as unobtrusively as possible.' *Right!*

Researcher: 'What if you mispronounce somebody's name?'

Shy: 'Well, I'd probably just say "Excuse me" and continue with what I'd been saying.' *Right!*

Even if you know the correct answers (and you do!), panic prevents you from thinking of them at the moment events are unfolding. While your spilled water streams towards a colleague's lap, you feel you're tied to your chair.

Write Your Own Horror Story

I'm sure you are aware that visualization is not just for sports psychologists to get their clients to go for the gold. It's how you gain confidence. It can also help you do the coolest thing when you face a calamity.

Let's say you must attend a business dinner. Before you leave, write a horror story of all the ways you could make an utter fool of yourself. *What if I burp audibly? What if I break a glass. What if I spill my soup?*

Step One: Upon finishing your frightening list, ask yourself what someone *should* do after burping, breaking, or spilling. When you think about it *unemotionally*, you know precisely how to handle it.

Step Two: Choose one of the embarrassing scenarios and say the correct answer to yourself. Better yet, say it out loud.

When your emotions aren't mucking you up, you probably know it. (If not, there is help in SHYBUSTER 60.)

Step Three: Close your eyes and 'see' yourself making the blooper. Then visualize yourself taking precisely the action you came up with. Continue with the next, the next, and the next – until you've chased all the butterflies away.

SHYBUSTER 59:
Make a Mental Movie of Your Cool Moves

In the remote possibility that some kind of *faux pas* transpires, you don't need to panic or think 'What do I do now?' Thanks to your visualization, your body goes on auto-pilot and you sail through the situation with panache.

Inevitably, of course, a situation will arise where neither a Sure nor a Shy would spontaneously know what to do. Let's say you drop your fork at a dinner party. Those nasty inner voices taunt you:

Hey, butterfingers, pick the thing up.

C'mon, loser, haven't you got any class? Call the waiter.

Stupid, that would only call attention to your blooper. Let it lie there.

Wait a minute, wuss, kick it under the table so nobody sees it. Then finish your roast beef with your spoon.

Someone spots the frozen hysteria on your face and turns towards you. 'Is anything wrong?' Now you want to die.

I once faced the fork predicament and, without the proper utensil, didn't eat another morsel. When I got home, munching on a sandwich, I pulled a dusty Amy Vanderbilt etiquette book off the shelf – written in 1956. Eureka! On a page yellowed with age, I found the answer. (It's option two – call the waiter over and ask for another fork.)

What If I Don't Know What to Do?

Until you become a certified Sure and trust your own instincts, an etiquette book covers most possible social 'catastrophes'. I know, 'etiquette' sounds stuffy. But it's no longer just 'What should the mother of the bride wear?' or 'What kind of personal stationery should I have?' My favourite, *Miss Manner's Guide for the Turn of the Millennium* has chapters like 'How Not to Stand Around Looking Stupid'.[3]

Guys, don't skip this one. It's for you, too.

SHYBUSTER 60:
What the Manners Mavens Say

A good etiquette book is salvation for Shys when faced with dreadful dilemmas like 'What do I do when a tabletop tidal-wave from my water heads her way?' With the confidence of knowing what the experts suggest, your anxiety evaporates. You won't worry that the Etiquette Police will arrest you. Or worse, that people will laugh at you.

Parents, there is no need to rip Lemony Snicket out of your kid's little hands and shove *Amy Vanderbilt's Everyday Etiquette* under their nose. Instead, teach them early what to do in a variety of social situations. Compliment them when they do it correctly. Praise them profusely when they cover a sneeze or say, 'I'm sorry, Mummy' as their biscuit goes rolling across the floor.

Rhesus monkeys are shy, similar to human babies. Same patterns, same percentages.[4]

That's definitely of no help to you. I just thought it was interesting. Besides, who wouldn't be shy if they had a red bottom as big and ugly as a Rhesus monkey's?

take a bite out of shyness for lunch

A Very Healthy Diet

Another SOS exercise: Every lunch-hour, take on an additional tiny challenge. Suppose you eat at a company cafeteria:

Monday's midday challenge: Ring up an hour before to ask what today's special is.

Tuesday: Ask if you can substitute mashed potatoes for the sweetcorn.

Wednesday: Stop by a colleague's table and ask If they'd recommend the ham sandwich they're eating.

Thursday: Invite someone to sit with you in the cafeteria.

Friday: Ask if you can join several people you know at a table.

The possibilities are endless. So are the benefits. But you must keep up the routine. It's like body-building. A heavy workout once a week can break your back. Do a light workout every day and you're soon lifting normally back-breaking weights effortlessly.

Likewise, a big challenge just once a week can break your confidence. A light challenge every day and you're soon throwing your own weight around effortlessly.

SHYBUSTER 61:
Eat Your Shyness

Make a 'Sure' move every lunch-hour. Punish yourself if you don't. Let's say your challenge *du jour* was to invite someone to join you. Make a rule. You don't do it, you don't eat. You'll be amazed what an effective motivator hunger is.

download confidence into your eardrums

Turn Off the Music, Turn On the Confidence

While driving, do you hear these lyrics running through your head?:

I acted so shy. I know everybody noticed.

I don't know anybody there. I'll just stand around looking like an idiot.

It was horrible. I couldn't even look him in the eyes.

I can't ask her for a date. She'd laugh at me.

People tell you, 'Well, just stop thinking about yourself.' That's like saying, 'Don't think about a pink hippopotamus.' Impossible!

Some Shys say listening to music takes concentration off themselves. But, by the second song, it's just background music for the treacherous thoughts. 'Fight fire with fire' the saying goes. Likewise, the only way to fight words is with words.

Millions of positive words, on CD or cassette, are just waiting to enter your ears and drive those negative thoughts away.

" Recently, instead of playing music in my car, I put in some of those CDs where someone is talking about positive things. My favourite, of course, is your 'Conversation Confidence', then Brian Tracy's 'The

Psychology of Sales'. They've been very helpful with my job but, most important, they keep my mind off myself except for planning to do some of the positive and profitable stuff you and Tracy suggest."

WILL – CHICAGO, ILLINOIS

Audio Track to Confidence

It was kind of Will to mention my *Conversation Confidence* audio, but I suggest also listening to programmes that have nothing to do with confidence or social skills. Find an audio on how to fix your car, feng shui your home, find bargains to wear, or get rid of junk. The list is endless. In addition to learning new skills, every audio you listen to makes you a more interesting person and gives you more to talk about.

SHYBUSTER 62:
Listen to the Voices in Your Head

Thousands of audio programmes are sitting on library or shop shelves. Or hiding on the net just waiting to be downloaded. Start a healthy mental diet to force poisonous thinking out.

Don't forget the plethora of books on tape or CD. They fill your mind with engrossing stories to replace the horror stories of your imagined screw-ups.

---

section XI

sex and the single shy

there are no love 'guarantees'

On your first date, you can't say to someone, 'If we have a second date, do you promise to love me and be faithful to me for ever?' Yet that is what many Shys subconsciously want. There is one book, more than any other, that is literally within arm's reach of most psychiatrists and psychologists. It is the *Statistical Manual of Mental Disorders* – the 'Bible' as they often refer to it. Whenever a question comes up, their hand shoots across their desk to grab it. A quick flip of the pages and they have the answer to any question they are asked.

The third revised edition describes one quality which, when it comes to relationships, many Shys share:

> **They are hypersensitive to potential rejection, humiliation, or shame. Social avoidants are unwilling to enter into situations unless given unusually strong guarantees of uncritical acceptance.**[1]

Intellectually, of course, we know there are no 'guarantees' in love for Shys, Sures, nor the rich nor famous. (Especially the last category!) Practically all Shys are capable of falling in love, being deeply loved, and having fulfilling relationships.

However, because Shys are super-sensitive, they may be a bit slower to achieve their goal, and they should play the game more carefully to avoid being hurt. The chapters that follow contain warnings of a few common pitfalls, and suggestions on how to avoid them.

a dangerous
dating game
for shys

Opportunity or Trap?

We are fortunate to be living in this most exciting era of all time. Simple words can never describe how phenomenal the Internet is. But with every humongous silver lining, a tiny cloud can be found in the middle. And this is a very dark one for Shys.

It's spectacular that you can research anything on the web and find like-minded people. Sadly, you seldom meet them face to face.

Spectacular that you can telecommute to work. Sadly, that doesn't involve chatting around the water-cooler.

Spectacular that you can learn just about anything on the web – except social skills. Sadly, that's just what Shys need.

❝ I am not in the least bit shy when I communicate with people by e-mail. I have been doing it for three years now and have communicated with lots of great guys. I can take all the time I want to get my thoughts together, correct them, and then reread it to make sure it sounds like what I genuinely mean to say. This helps someone to get to

know the real me and I can get to know the real them."

SARAH – NORTHAMPTON, MASSACHUSETTS

But can you, Sarah? Unfortunately, you don't have the luxury to think five minutes before you respond face to face. You can't push backspace/delete in conversation. Personality and 'chemistry' don't travel well in cyberspace.

Also, consider that some of those 'great guys' you're communicating with may be misrepresenting themselves. Do you think every tall, dark, handsome, brilliant, loving, caring and honourable man who e-mails you really is tall, dark, handsome, brilliant, loving, caring, and honourable?

I e-mailed Sarah to ask what some of these great guys were really like. She told me she hasn't had any face-to-face meetings yet. Hmm.

It's also spectacular that you can find partners on the web. Sadly, Shys don't do well in the on-line love game. They often hide behind it and never meet their cyber-pen pal. If they do, and it doesn't click, they can plummet more deeply into shyness. It can even shake the confidence of a Sure.

A good friend of mine, Ann, is a good-looking woman – fabulous dresser, professional, smart – and she knows it. She hasn't yet found Mr Right, though, so she put an ad on a dating site. She got several dozen responses, e-mailed six, had phone conversations and exchanged photos with four, agreed to meet two.

The rendezvous with the first was at a well-known restaurant. The meeting time was 7 p.m. She told her blind date she'd be wearing a yellow suit and a long orange scarf so there could be no way he'd miss her.

Ann arrived on time and waited at the bar. She thought several men walking by looked like the photo she'd received, but she couldn't be sure.

By 7.45, she paid for her drink and left.

At 8 my phone rang. Ann's voice was bordering on the hysterical, 'That's the first time in all my life I've ever been stood up!' Ann was usually pretty confident, but I knew that the experience had taken a big bite out of her ego when she said, 'Leil, he must have been there, taken one look at me, and decided not to approach.'

Computer dating clobbered her again. She met a doctor on line and they made a date at a posh restaurant. Over cocktails, potential Mr Right told her an emergency had come up at the hospital and he wouldn't be able to stay for dinner.

'He apologized,' Ann said, 'and told me the bill would be "taken care of". What an insult! Did he think I was some pauper? I know he was just buying me off because he didn't like me.'

If Ann didn't have a healthy self-image to start with, these experiences would have been almost fatal to her confidence.

SHYBUSTER 63:

Computer Dating Is a Sure's Game

On-line dating is one of those 'Proceed at your own risk' situations. The first part of the trip is fun when you're e-mailing. But the road can take a dangerous turn when you meet. Your ego crashes if you are rejected.

When you become a Sure, the cheap shots will feel like a water gun on a duck's back. For now, weigh the advantages and dangers carefully before you click 'Send'.

The same holds for speed-dating. Not being put on someone's 'Want to meet' list is disappointing to a Sure. It could be devastating for a Shy because they take rejection so personally.

Your call. However, you might consider leaving speed-dating to the Super-Sures and egomaniacs for now. There will be plenty of time to enjoy these new twists on the old dating game when you've got your diploma from Stamp Out Shyness school.

oversexed or underconfident?

Shy Baby Sister or Class Slut?

On a trip to my home town I ran into Lynda, a girl who'd lived across the street from me when I was in high school. We had a great time laughing about all the neighbourhood 'characters' we'd known and about the kids we'd babysat for. Lynda had a sister called Carrina who was extremely good looking. Often I'd heard her coming home from a date in the wee hours in the morning. I asked Lynda, 'How is Carrina? Does she still live in Bethesda?'

Lynda's face fell. 'Nearby,' she answered, mentioning a downtrodden part of Washington DC.

Seeing Lynda's dismay, I thought it prudent to change the subject, 'How about your Mom? She doing well?'

'Oh she's great, but ... Carrina has her problems.' I was silent, realizing that Lynda did indeed want to talk about her sister.

She showed me a photo from her wallet of Carrina, a man, and three kids. 'Carrina's living with another guy now.' I couldn't believe it was the same girl. She looked haggard and almost older than Lynda's age and mine put together.

'Uh, cute kids,' was the only thing I could think of to say.

'All different dads. I know what you're thinking, Leil.'

I was. 'What happened?'

'Carrina was a bright girl and she had terrific looks going for her.'

'She really did. I saw how popular she was. Lots of dates.'

'Too many. But that was because she'd "put out" for any guy who dated her, even once.' Lynda gave a wry smile. 'I guess she was just the girl who couldn't say "No".'

'I don't understand,' I said. 'Was she just oversexed?'

'No, underconfident. Still is. In fact, she told me she doesn't even enjoy the sex. But she's so shy she doesn't want to say "No" to any guy. She's afraid he'll give her hassle. So she just goes along with anything the guy wants to avoid arguments. I think she feels so worthless she figures she could never get love in any other way. So she mistakes sex for affection.'

SHYBUSTER 64:
Don't Get Caught in the Sex/Love Trap

Love usually culminates in sex. But don't let loneliness convince you that it works the other way, too. Everyone should think carefully before deciding to have sex – Shys especially. You are more sensitive than most people. Therefore, more vulnerable and more easily hurt. Sex is a big step, and the last thing you need right now is heartbreak. Just look before you leap into bed with someone.

Lynda looked at the photo of her sister sadly. 'She got known as the "school slut". None of the girls wanted to be seen with her, and neither did the guys. They wanted to screw her at night but not talk to her at school. Pretty soon it got to the point where'd they'd pick her up, take her to their place, do it and bring her back afterward. Sometimes they'd even send her back on the bus.'

'And she was such a sweet kid ...'

Fear of real relationships can drive Shys to less healthy sexual outlets like promiscuity, telephone sex lines, Internet pornography and compulsive masturbation.[1]

Intimacy Is Not the Problem

One would think that having sex in a relationship would be tough for Shys. For some who have performance problems, it can be. However, once a Shy is in a good relationship, sex is not usually a problem. Dr Bernardo Carducci, who has spent 25 years studying shyness, has found that only a small percentage of Shys has a problem with sex once he or she has a partner.[2]

I once worked on a charity event with an Indian woman named Aastha. We became quite close and, during our long hours being together, talked about everything imaginable – including her sex life.

She was recently married to her husband, Stephen. She said, 'He was in a drawing class I was taking. He never talked to anybody.' She smiled. 'I thought he was sort of cute so I said "Hi" to him once. I think he was pleased.

'For the next several classes we talked a little bit. Then there was a Modigliani exhibition I wanted to see and I asked if he would join me.

'He did and one thing led to another and we started dating. He is still a little shy – but he sure isn't shy about one thing.' She looked around to make sure no one was listening. 'He is unbelievable!'

There was no doubt what she was talking about.

It's Not That Easy for a Shy Guy

Unfortunately, not all Shys are fortunate enough to find a partner. The police, in interrogating the Madam of a 'house of ill repute' after it was busted in San Francisco, heard some surprising stories. Miss Kitty (yes, that's really what she called herself) always took the money from the customers before the 'services' were delivered.

She reported, 'Some customers would pay, and then were too shy to go upstairs.'

The Delancy Street Foundation in San Francisco interviewed a diverse selection of prostitutes, from 'higher class' call-girls who worked on referral to streetwalkers.[3] These ladies of the night reported that 60 per cent of their clients were shy. Even more surprising is that half the prostitutes described *themselves* as shy. They were confident only when they were 'playing the role' of prostitute.

Shy men, you don't have the confidence to approach a woman you like. And shy women, due to your insecurity you don't flirt with a man to encourage his advance.

The result? Many shy men marry women who are not

their first choice, because a confident woman set her sights on him. And shy women often 'settle' for someone who is not Mr Right, just Mr OK.

> **"** I realized that if my wife weren't the aggressive type, we would never have got together. We were set up on a blind date. I golfed with a man whose wife worked with her. Our first kiss was entirely at my wife's instigation. While I was attracted to her, if she hadn't made it so blatantly clear that she liked me, I probably would have assumed she didn't and never bothered calling her again. **"**
>
> DAVID – GREAT FALLS, MONTANA

being shy and
gay is lonely

I am not qualified to write this important chapter. A reader named Paul is. I want to share his letter with you. It is poignant and gently chides me for something I plead guilty to.

>**"I** have a tremendous lack of self-esteem that has plagued me for many years. I know I must improve upon my self-confidence. First I want to tell you that your books and recordings have changed my life. I find myself agreeing with you often, constantly seeing myself and my problems and *faux pas* in your stories and descriptions.
>
>However, in that search to improve I find I have to chart my own course even more so than many of your readers. I wanted to let you know in the hope that you might think a little about how to address my problems and those of millions of other people.
>
>You see – and I'd be surprised if you hadn't guessed this already – I'm gay. I'm a 42 year old male – who for the most part of his life has been unable to find a partner or

even very many people to date. I know many people think most gay men don't have a big problem in relating to other gay men. And you may even have the impression that gay life is just hopping from one bed to another – or from one partner to another. But this isn't true for a lot of us – especially the older people and people not raised in big cities or the more progressive areas of the country.

I'd venture to guess that even though probably 10 per cent of the population is gay or bi, we need help in figuring out how to find a good partner.

As wonderful as your books and CDs are, they are structured for the heterosexual side of the equation. I do understand that's what you are and it constitutes the majority of your readers. And I certainly wouldn't ask you to put out a series targeting gays (and/or lesbians, and all the other colours in the diverse rainbow).

But please, consider letting your readers know that we feel the same way, and have even greater challenges because we are gay. I know I'm not the only shy gay out here – and we need the help as much as anyone else. Especially the gay man or woman in smaller towns and rural areas who may not be able to find counsellors or therapists who can or will deal with gays.

And many of them consider themselves isolated and friendless and are in need of help when it comes to personal relationship skills.

Most of the gays I know, and chat with on line, both in the US and throughout the world, really do want to find someone to love who loves us back. And someone who wants to be in a long-term relationship. I'm sure I'm not the only gay male in the US who doesn't want to grow old alone."

PAUL M. – DALLAS

Thank you, Paul, for reminding me of my egregious omission and taking the time to write to me.

English is a bulky language and all writers struggle with the words 'he' and 'she' when it could be either. I also find that reading 'potential love partner' too often becomes ponderous. Linguistically, gender-specific words flow more smoothly. Words like 'opposite sex', although often not appropriate, are part of our language.

Paul and all readers, please understand that when I use these words, it is merely for linguistic simplicity. I am hoping that our language changes to encompass everyone. And, of course to make it easier for us writers! Please know, too, that everything I say about overcoming shyness naturally will work for gay readers as well.

relationship rehearsals

A Mind-Boggling Question

Can you answer these questions?

What is the difference between a beautiful woman and a not-so-beautiful one?

Answer: One is beautiful and the other one isn't.

What's the difference between a prince and a frog?

Answer: One's a prince and the other is a frog.

Why should you be nervous on a date with the first if not the second? We always assume that attractive people are 'different'. Not true. Having worked around plenty of beautiful men and women as a Pan Am flight attendant, I know the only difference is that the beautiful ones act a little more haughtily. And even that's not always true. Some of the best-looking people are tormented by insecurity. (And some of the less obviously attractive ones are the most beautiful inside.)

" I was a fashion model for a few years
and that didn't help my confidence at all.
I would go to a party and men would be
hitting on me. But I'd just smile and say
'Hi,' and that would be it. If someone
asked me something, I would give a quick

answer, and then wouldn't have a clue what else to say.

Men would ask me out on dates and I'm sure that they felt lucky to be going out with this model, but they quickly would realize that I was so shy that I was the most boring date they'd ever had and could hardly wait for it to end!"

ALEXIA – CHICAGO, ILLINOIS

Shys, if it's any consolation, all over the world even confidant people go to pieces around their more beautiful counterparts. Here's one from Russia ... with (lost) love.

" I have always been assured of myself in most situations, but there are some dreaded desperate times, especially around a beautiful woman, when shyness conquers me and my mind goes through a transformation, a switch from cool and collected to hot and broken down.

Six years ago there was a young woman who worked in a shop next-door to my office. I looked at her through the window almost daily as I passed her shop. I developed an interest in her and always thought to myself how I would I act when I finally meet her, what would I say? I prepared my poetic opening lines, my smooth Romeo approach, and my stunning gaze. I imagined her responses, and how I would smoothly navigate through them to finally ask her out on a date.

Well, it all seemed just fine and dandy until I actually met her. My speech stumbled, my palms got sweaty, and my words magically started missing syllables. She thought it was cute that my face turned red. But then I knocked down the entire display of women's shoes in her shop and quickly left. I will never forget that moment and am still hating myself for being so flustered.**"**

BORIS – MOSCOW, RUSSIA

The sad part is that Shys often remember an unspoken encounter for years and torture themselves about 'the one that got away':

" It seems that only losers ask me out and I don't want to waste my time with them. I really think I deserve better. Anyway, there is this man Carl I sort of had a crush on even though we had seldom spoken. He works on the 18th floor of my office building and I work on the 20th. I think he liked me because he used to smile at me whenever he saw me. Carl happened to get into the elevator one time when I was riding down and I didn't know what to say to him. It was a very long ride. He smiled at me and said, 'You're very quiet today.' I hate it when people say that.

I just looked down and then he said, 'Are you shy?' I wanted to tell him 'No' but I was so nervous I couldn't. He then said some friends were going to the game that weekend and would I join him? I wanted so much to say 'Yes' but I'd never been to a football game and was worried I wouldn't know how to act. The elevator reached the ground floor just then and I just ran out the door. It was horrible. I can hardly face him at work anymore and he doesn't smile at me anymore."

LAUREL – SMYRNA, DELAWARE

Do Some Practice Dates

Begin dating someone who does *not* intimidate you. Laurel, it sounds like you could have gone to a football game with any number of men ('losers' who ask you out) just for the experience. Even frogs speak football. Learning how to jump up and down and yell for the team would probably have made you confident enough to say 'Yes' to Carl.

Please, dear readers, forgive me if this sounds callous. Men, there are plenty of women you would call 'dogs' who are dying to go out with you. Take one to a nice restaurant, compliment her and ask her questions about her life.

Get practice tasting the wine, putting her coat around her shoulders, offering your arm as you walk to the car. Not only is it practice for taking out the stunner. You may find you're enjoying yourself.

Likewise, women, the pond is full of frogs you wouldn't want as a life partner. But give the boys a thrill and go out with a few of them as 'practice dates'. If they don't ask you, you ask them. This is the 21st century and the old mores are fading fast.

Mr and Ms Shy, when you gain confidence to go for better pickings, please be gentle and loving with the feelings of the dud you are dumping.

Now go find someone a bit more intimidating. Repeat this sequence until you are finally confident around Mr or Ms Most Desired Person.

A Caution and a Gift

May I give you a caution, and a gift? They are one and the same.

First the caution: Don't 'settle' out of comfort if you genuinely feel your practice date is not for you.

Now the gift: There is a good chance you will genuinely start to like or fall in love with one of your 'stepping stones'. He or she may be a loving person, appreciate you, make you feel good about yourself, and be a marvellous mate. Don't ignore this diamond in the rough. You might be much happier with this mate than if you stay on the lonely path searching for the impossible dream.

A study on couples' compatibility attests to this. You will have a much happier long-term relationship with someone more equal in looks, money and personality than you would be with the gorgeous, rich life and soul of the party.

The more equitable the partners' assets, the happier they are. If one of the partners is much richer or more attractive, there is an imbalance. Discontent soon sets in.[1]

the lovin' is easy.
it's getting there
that's hard

Now For Some Good News About Love (About Time!)

Of course there are love-traps than can be fatal to a Shy's relationship. Due to your sensitivity, you probably have a greater need to connect with a loved one. And you probably have had a longer and lonelier search.

Shy people typically wed later than those who are not shy or anxious around other people.[1]

However, when you do find a partner, you are usually capable of a deeper love than non-Shys. If the love is carefully controlled and reciprocated, it can bring both of you manifold pleasures often out of the reach of Sures who have dated extensively and had many intimate relationships.

When Shys finally do find their life partner, their spouses usually highly appreciate their qualities. Husbands and wives of Shys described their spouses' qualities as 'modest', 'cautious', 'dignified', 'sensitive' and 'sincere'.[2]

You must treat love as the treasure it is. There are potential perils for Shys. But if you are aware of them, the previous anguish you have suffered can be counterbalanced by incomparable joy.

Why do Shys, especially Highly Sensitive Shys, fall in love more intensely? Shys are more sensitive to their inner lives, and when someone enters that circle they become particularly precious. Some Shys love their partner as much as or more than they love themselves.

Is it a healthy love? Or does it stem from lack of self-esteem and needing to be 'completed' by another? Sometimes. Does a Shy fall in love with the first person who says they love them? Sometimes. Does a Shy fall so deeply in love that it can be suffocating for their partner? Sometimes. Can a Shy's marriage deteriorate because they are not willing to socialize or do things with their partner? Sometimes. Can a Shy be tormented by fears and fantasies of their partner's infidelity? Sometimes. But so can Sures.

Now, however, you have an advantage. If you are aware that you are more susceptible to these pitfalls, you can take more care to avoid them – and thus have longer and happier relationships. I wish you the love you so richly deserve.

shall I put on a big act?

Voice Quality Counts, Too

What quality reveals shyness most? You've probably said 'eye-contact', and you are right. However, many Shys aren't aware that our voices run a photo-finish second. The volume, speed and timbre of your voice is a measure of your assurance or lack of it.

To discover the significance of someone's voice in social situations, researchers recorded a group of students who were popular with their colleagues and dated a lot. They also recorded the voices of students who did not have many friends. One the biggest differences was their voices.[1]

The popular students had more volume, resonance and musicality. The voices of the less-accepted ones were filled with hesitant pauses. *How* you say something deafens people to *what* you are saying.

When you speak in a hushed voice, all they hear is, 'What I'm saying is not very important.'

When you pause, they hear, 'I don't have my thoughts together.'

When you hesitate, they hear, 'I can't keep my mind on what you're saying because I'm too distracted by wondering what you think of me.'

When you speak too fast, they hear, 'I'd better race through this sentence before I get distracted thinking about myself again.'

Confirmation That I Was 'Cured'

After using most of the SHYBUSTERs we've discussed, I felt cured of the agonizing condition called Shyness. The 'coffee, tea, or me' routine helped my shyness subside tremendously. Pampering hundreds of airline passengers weekly for two years didn't leave much time to worry about the impression I was making.

Due to an ecstatic experience which I'll reveal later I felt I had graduated. However, I craved one more clash with crowds to confirm that my shyness was gone for good. For two summers, I took a job as Social Hostess on a cruise ship.

To get my coveted job, I used SHYBUSTER 19 and pumped my energy level sky-high walking through each interviewer's door.

Then, as SHYBUSTER 35 directs, I interviewed with four other cruise ship lines before I went for the one I really wanted.

As the ship's Social Hostess it was my job to hold a singles get-together at every departure. After the confetti settled on the deck and the waving well-wishers on the shore disappeared in the distance, I'd welcome the singles into the disco. Every week I saw the guys grin and the girls glower when they realized the female/male ratio on a ship is three to one. (Women, if you go on a cruise, don't expect the Love Boat. Single men, it's the Love Boat!) One time, as the women began descending on the few men like vultures on a lamb chop, I saw them miss the one fellow sitting alone in the corner.

It Takes One to Spot One

I went over to greet him and he gave me a hesitant 'Hello' in a volume a librarian would approve of. Most people don't instantly recognize a Shy but, as one who'd fought the bitter battle, I saw shy written all over him.

I knew there wasn't much I could do for him in one week, but I wanted to give it a try. I invited Ned to have coffee on deck with me the next morning. He seemed more at ease when I told him about my successful struggle with shyness. He told me he was thinking of taking speech classes because his voice was so weak.

When I was in high school, I too thought that would help. It just so happened my mother was a speech therapist, one of the best in the country I might brag. I asked Mama for speech lessons.

'Why, Leilie? You don't have any speech problems.'

'Mother,' I said, 'I want to learn to speak up and not sound so shy.'

She told me speech lessons wouldn't help. She was right. Research has subsequently shown that this is not the right road.[2] However, there is another road to having a smooth, strong and confident voice. In fact, it's a super-highway.

'Ned, may I suggest a way which has proven far more effective?'

He looked at me sceptically. 'What is it?'

I told him.

'I'll think it over,' he mumbled.

On Saturday the cruise was over. I said 'Goodbye' to the passengers and gave Ned a hug as he headed down the gangway.

'Ned, stay in touch!' I called after him.

I didn't expect to hear from Ned, but the first time we docked in New York the following summer, the steward delivered a dozen roses to my cabin. The card read, 'Love from Ned, your shy passenger from last year. Can you meet me on the dock? I have some exciting news.'

I descended the gangway planning to search for my timid friend on the edge of the crowd. Above the clamour I heard 'Leil, Leil, over here.' An energetic fellow waving both arms came running towards the ship.

'Ned?' I gasped. This lively guy couldn't be nervous Ned.

Sitting in a nearby coffee shop, he told me he had taken my suggestion – acting classes – seriously. He'd been in three shows already and was now playing the role of Stanley Kowalski in *A Streetcar Named Desire*. Imagining Ned on stage in a torn T-shirt, slapping a beer on the table and hollering for his wife was mind-boggling.

'Leil,' he said, 'it is amazing.' He told me he'd learned to project his voice to the last row. He was directed to use big gestures. 'That and making eye-contact with all the performers was a life-changer.' Ned looked exuberant. 'I learned that if I can take on three distinct personalities for an audience of 100, I can take on the role of "confident person" for a mere 20 or so people at a party.'

I was thrilled for Ned and have subsequently suggested acting lessons to students in my shyness seminars. Sometimes they say, 'But if I were just "pretending" to be an extroverted person offstage, it wouldn't be really "me".'

Of course, at first you won't feel like the old shy you. But isn't that what you're trying to escape? You want to become the new confident you.

You will be yourself in all the important ways – your beliefs, your values, your principles. You will simply have the personality and confidence to speak up more often, in a stronger voice so people listen.

Shy people are often concerned whether or not their actions reflect their real selves. Like a method actor, you must learn to dissolve the bond between the so-called real you and the role you play. Let your actions speak for themselves and eventually they will be speaking for you.[3]

SHYBUSTER 65:
Act Your Way to Confidence

Being somebody else on stage does wonders for playing the most important role of your life – your most extroverted self.

After using larger movements, a louder voice and good eye-contact on stage, you'll be just as dynamic at the last-night closing party – and in many more social situations to come.

" One of the things that I think really helped my shyness was when my best friend joined the drama club at school and wanted me to join, too. We did some scenes and in one of them I was cast as this very flashy, bitchy woman. I was scared to death at first but, after having that personality on stage, it was a little easier to exert myself in real life. "

ALISA – WASHINGTON, DC

section XII

shy no more

graduation day

From Frightened Rabbit to Bold Bunny

Just as some Shys remember the ghastly moment their shyness started, many can speak of a glorious moment when they realized it was gone. Some can point to a pivotal moment when they can say, 'I'm free – I'm no longer shy!' For me, it happened after Daffy and I worked a trip to London. While chatting in the galley, Daf said she was proud of me because I was looking right into passengers eyes when I asked, 'Would you like coffee now? Or perhaps you would prefer tea?' (Flight attendants spoke in complete sentences in those days.)

I felt like a successful student. But, on a London layover, she gave me another of those familiar 'I've-got-something-up-my-sleeve' expressions.

'Uh, oh,' I said. But this time I really didn't mind because her self-styled 'graduated exposure' therapy was working wonderfully. She whispered, 'We're going someplace tonight and you're going to be just as pleasant to the people there as you were to my mother's Greek friends – and as friendly as you now are to passengers.'

I was feeling pretty cocky about my progress. 'Sure, Daf, anywhere you want.'

After we'd slept the jet-lag off, did a little shopping and had a bite to eat, we hopped on a bus. Daffy still hadn't told me where she was taking me. At each stop I'd press my nose against the window and ask, 'Here?'

'Nope.'

'Here?'

'Nope.'

The next stop was in front of the old Playboy Club on Park Lane.

'Here?!' I joked.

'Yes!'

I held on to my seat. 'Oh no, Daffy. You're not getting me in there.'

She pulled me up. 'Oh yes, I am.'

'Do they allow women without bunny tails in?' I mumbled as she dragged me to the door.

As the maitre d' wended his way through the crowd to our table, I noticed a number of men momentarily ungluing their eyes from the bunnies' fluffy tails and silk ears to look at us. I thought back to the Greek restaurant and, just as I did then, I sat up straight, brushed my hair back, and even smiled at a few of the men.

One of the Playboy bunnies must have noticed my excitement. While doing the graceful 'bunny dip' serving us our drinks, she whispered to me, 'I have an extra pair of bunny ears in the back if you'd like to wear them.' Daffy gasped when I gleefully placed them on my head.

'Hey, cool it,' Daffy said. 'Now you're going too far!'

I really was, and it was thrilling. I had gone from anonymous bunny in the Christmas pageant to blatant bunny in the Playboy Club. I wanted to dance and shout, 'I'm free – I'm no longer shy!'

At that instant, I started planning to give a little surprise party for Daffy's birthday. Now, *that* was confirmation that I'd won the battle.

SHYBUSTER 66:
Give Yourself a Graduation Party

When you've finished all the SHYBUSTERS, celebrate by actually giving a little party. Plan an office birthday celebration for a colleague. Or invite the boys to your place for a World Cup bash. Nobody will know, as you lift your glass, that you're happily toasting your own Success Over Shyness. You've gone from Party Panic to Party Planner.

Several men at the Playboy Club came to our table to chat. While they were ordering drinks for us, Daffy whispered, 'Go, girl. Nobody would ever guess you were shy.'

I winked at her, 'I'll just keep faking it till I make it.' But I wasn't faking it anymore.

Soon you too will be wearing your graduation cap, though probably not silk ears like mine. But choose a baseball cap, beret, helmet, turban, tiara or just an invisible crown. You will silently and ecstatically shout, 'I'm free! No more shyness!' Nobody will hear you, of course, just your new confident self – and that's the most important person.

notes

Cheryl's Full Letter

" Dear Leil,
I have struggled with 'shyness' all of
my life, feeling like I'm marching to a
different drummer than most of the world.
I couldn't understand why many of my
schoolmates and co-workers enjoyed
talking with lots of people and spending
large amounts of time visiting when I
preferred just one or two close friends,
more intimate settings, and deeper
conversation. I couldn't figure out why I
would rather remain in the background
and think about a topic before speaking,
while others would vocalize their
thoughts without restraint. I couldn't
fathom how people who became my
closest and dearest friends would later
tell me that they thought I was 'cold' or
'aloof' upon first impression but realized I
was 'anything but' after they got to know
me. I was very intelligent, always an
honours student and later an excellent

businessperson, and truly liked people. But I couldn't seem to get the hang of the whole socializing bit. I wondered if something was 'wrong' with me.

I began the process of self-discovery and research several years ago, and I'm convinced more than ever that shyness is a symptom and introversion is the source. Introversion is not a disease, quite the contrary, but it can certainly be viewed as a handicap in an extroverted world.

In order to be effective in my job (I'm in a very extroverted job that involves talking to people most of the day) I've learned a number of things that have helped me to accept and 'manage' my introversion.

1. Nothing is wrong with me. I have lots to offer to others because I'm an introvert, cannot, and should not, change who I am. But I can become more effective in my interactions with others.

2. I have learned to be extrovert if needed. If I anticipate a period of extroversion that involves a difficult discussion or confrontation, I will often rehearse it mentally or in writing. However, I must schedule a counterbalance (quiet and solace) following times of extroversion in order to recharge my batteries.

3. I must assess the 'audience' with which I am interacting and adapt my behaviour accordingly when dealing with an extrovert. I should not expect the extrovert to adapt to me. I adapt to them to communicate better.

4. I will place myself in situations that require me to strengthen my weak extroversion 'muscle'. For example, I volunteer for leadership positions for which I am uncomfortable in order to develop more expertise in dealing with others. I force myself to speak up in meetings rather than sitting by passively.

5. I look for tips and techniques to help me feel at ease making the small talk that extroverts enjoy. When the necessity arises, I can become a 'pseudoextrovert'. Much to my pleasure, once I get the conversation started, the extrovert will typically do the majority of talking. Because I genuinely like people, I listen and appreciate that I've got to know someone better or made a new friend. I would have missed out on that opportunity if I did not make the first approach.

6. I encourage my children's extroversion even though it is uncomfortable at times. However, I also try to teach them to be sensitive to the

introverts in their lives, like their mother, and to recognize that a person's need for times of solitude is just another way of approaching life.

Thank you for your work in this area. I've gained so much from reading your materials and look forward with anticipation to your new book on shyness.

CHERYL MOSTROM

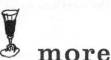

more
self-knowledge
questions

1. What is 'honour' to me? Am I honourable?
2. What's really important to me?
3. What motivates people?
4. What is an ideal relationship to me?
5. What would retirement mean to me?
6. How do I feel about what's happening in the environment now?
7. Who has been the greatest influence on my life?
8. What would/does having children mean to me?
9. Who is the God of my understanding?
10. What is my definition of 'success' for me? Am I successful?
11. If I had only a few months to live, how would I spend it?
12. What do I think the human brain is capable of?
13. If I won a ticket to travel anywhere in the world, where would I go?
14. Are things in life 'predestined'? Is there free will?
15. What really gets me angry? Why?
16. What does art mean to the world? To me?
17. What do I think the future of the computer is? The web?
18. What makes a leader?
19. Do I believe in the 'supernatural'?

20. What is my greatest success in life to date?
21. What is my favourite holiday? Why?
22. What do I think happens after death?
23. What is my favourite meal?
24. Would I die for something I believed in?
25. What influence did my parents have on me?
26. What are my favourite books? Why?
27. If I could be famous, what would I want to be famous for?
28. What do I think is the cause of most relationships failing?
29. What is my favourite song? Why?
30. If I could live in any era, which would it be? Why?
31. What does loyalty mean to me?
32. What do I think is our country's influence around the world?
33. What do I think about most when I'm just standing in a queue?
34. How do I feel about ageing?
35. What are the most comfortable clothes to me?
36. How do I feel about industrial air pollution vs progress?
37. What is one thing I learned this week?
38. If I could afford to collect anything, what would I collect?
39. Who is my best friend? Why?
40. Am I a morning, afternoon or night person?
41. What do I like to watch on television? Why?
42. What do I think about the relationship between government and religion?
43. How do I define 'spirituality'?

44. What are my top 10 favourite web pages? Why?
45. How do I believe the universe was created?
46. What's the best thing about being the age I am? The worst?
47. How are kids born now and growing up with the Internet going to be different?
48. What is my opinion of my hometown's most popular newspaper?
49. What new personal rituals would I like to create?
50. How do I feel about animal testing if used to create a product to help humans?
51. Did I have a happy childhood?
52. Do I think most people lie a little? A lot?
53. What was the happiest day of my life to date?
54. What is my purpose in life?
55. What is my worst fear?
56. Do I want big commercial chains like McDonalds or Starbucks in my town?
57. Can I tell if somebody is lying? How?
58. Do I procrastinate too much? If so, on what and why?
59. How do I feel about meditation?
60. How do I feel about the town I was born in? How has it changed?
61. If I could change just one thing in my life, what would it be?
62. What is my favourite cartoon, and why?
63. Is it important to get eight hours of sleep? Why?
64. What relevance do the ancient philosophers have for today's way of life?
65. What does democracy mean to me?

66. How do I feel about school reunions?
67. Do I have any limiting patterns? If so, what could I do to change them?
68. What role does music play in my life?
69. How do I feel about television advertising?
70. Am I a 'dog person', a 'cat person', or do I prefer any other animal as pets?
71. How do I feel about the institution of marriage, in general?
72. How do I feel about organized religion?
73. How do I feel about marriage for me? Will it/has it been good?
74. Am I superstitious? If so, about what – and why?
75. What was my first job, and what did it mean to me?
76. Do I tend to suffer more from claustrophobia or vertigo – or neither?
77. Do I think we should limit world population in some way?
78. Do I believe in unconditional love?
79. If I had to live life in confinement, how would I adjust?
80. Do I think people are basically good or bad?
81. Should infomercials be banned? Why?
82. What is my favourite sport to play? To watch?
83. What is my opinion of current film/TV stars?
84. How much do I believe of what I hear on TV newscasts?
85. What is my favourite dish? Favourite restaurant?
86. Should we have legislation limiting buying foreign products versus domestic?

87. Do I believe in the 'big bang' theory of the universe?

88. Whose cooking do I most prefer (Mine? Mum's? Someone else's?)

89. How do I feel about eating meat versus vegetarianism?

90. If asked, 'Who are you?' what would I answer?

91. Are political elections fair? Why?

92. Do I believe any of the popular diets work?

93. What world leader do I feel has had the most positive impact on humanity?

94. If I could speak another language, what would it be? Why?

95. Do 'nice guys' or 'nice girls' finish last?

96. How do I feel about assisted suicide?

97. Should people know their family tree? Why?

98. Who is my favourite singer? Why?

99. What is my favourite television show? Why?

100. Do I think volunteerism can really get things done?

101. What is my favourite subject to talk about?

102. If I were reincarnated as an animal, what would I be? Why?

103. What is my stand on abortion and right to life?

104. How do I feel about our educational system? Why?

105. How do I feel about 'finding love on line'?

106. How do I really feel about each of my family members?

107. Am I happy? Why?

108. How will or how does my life differ from my parents' lives?

109. Were/Are my parents happy?
110. What would/do I wish for my children?
111. Do I have a satisfying sex life? Why?
112. At what age should someone retire?
    How about me?
113. Am I happy with the wardrobe I have?
114. Do I prefer travelling by train, plane, bus or car?
    Why?
115. If I owned my own company, how would I
    reward my employees?
116. How do I feel about my life right now?

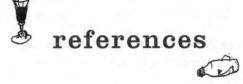

references

Don't Be an Avoidance Junkie

1. Beck, AT, Clark, DA. 'An Information Processing Model of Anxiety: Automatic and Strategic Processes', *Journal of Behavioral Research Therapy*, 1997, 35:49–58
2. Cappe, RF, Alden, LE. 'A Comparison of Treatment Strategies for Clients Functionally Impaired by Extreme Shyness and Social Avoidance', *Journal of Consulting and Clinical Psychology*, December 1986, 54(6):796–801

Welcome

1. Wells JC, Tien AY, Garrison R, Eaton WW. 'Risk Factors for the Incidence of Social Phobia as Determined by the Diagnostic Interview Schedule in a Population Based Study', *Acta Psychiatrica Scandinavica*, 1994, 90:84–90
2. Marshall, JR, MD. *Social Phobia*, Basic Books, New York, 1994
3. Pollack, M, MD, Simon, NM, MD, Otto, M, PhD. *Social Anxiety Disorder: Research and Practice*, Professional Publishing Group, New York, 2003
4. Ibid.

The Confidence Warm-up

1. Zimbardo, PG. *Shyness, What it Is, What to Do About it*, Perseus Books, Reading, Massachusetts, 1977

Take the 'Cot Test' to See if You Were Born Shy
1. Carducci, B, Zimbardo, P. 'Are You Shy?', *Psychology Today*, 2000
2. Kagan, J, Reznick, JS, Snidman, N. 'The Physiology and Psychology of Behavioral Inhibition in Children', *Journal of Child Development*, 1987, 58:1459–73
3. Kagan, J, Reznick, JS, Snidman, N. 'Biological Bases Of Childhood Shyness', *Science*, 1988, 240:167–71
4. Campbell, S. *Third and Long: Men's Playbook for Solving Marital/Relationship Problems and Building a Winning Team*, Authorhouse, 2005
5. Silverman, LK. 'Parenting Young Gifted Children' in Whitmore, JR (Ed.), *Intellectual Giftedness in Young Children*, The Haworth Press, New York, 1986
6. Aron, EN, PhD. *The Highly Sensitive Person in Love*, Broadway Books, New York, 2000

Did I 'Catch' a Dose of Shyness?
1. Cooper, PJ, Eke, M. 'Childhood Shyness and Maternal Social Phobia: a Community Study', *British Journal of Psychiatry*, 1999, 174:439–43
2. Zimbardo, PG. *Shyness, What it Is, What to Do About it*, Reading, Massachusetts,1977

Was it Bullies in Bygone Days?
1. Ost, L. 'Ways of Acquiring Phobias and Outcome of Behavioral Treatments', *Journal of Behavioral Research Therapy*, 1985, 23:683–9
2. Stemberger, R, Turner, S, Beidel, D, et al. 'Social Phobia, an Analysis of Possible Developmental Factors', *Journal of Abnormal Psychology*, 1995, 104:526–31

3. Taylor, AR. 'Predictors of Peer Rejection in Early
    Elementary Grades: Roles of Problem Behavior,
    Academic Achievement, and Teacher Preference',
    Journal of Clinical Child Psychology, 1989, 18:360–65
4. Ibid.

It Was All Mum and Dad's Fault

1. Chorpita, BF, Barlow, DH. 'The Development of Anxiety:
    the Role of Control in the Early Environment',
    Psychology Bulletin, 1998, 124:3–21
2. Belsky, J, Hsieh, K, Crnic, K. 'Mothering, Fathering, and
    Infant Negativity as Antecedents of Boy's Externalizing
    Problems and Inhibition at Age 3 Years: Differential
    Susceptibility to Rearing Experience?', *Developmental
    Psychopathology*, 1998, 10:301–19

Can People Tell I'm Shy

1. Kessler, RC, et al. 'Lifetime and 12-Month Prevalence of
    DSM-III-R Psychiatric Disorders in the United States',
    Archive General Psychiatry, 1994, 51:8–19
2. Zimbardo, P, PhD. 'The Social Disease Called Shyness',
    Psychology Today, 1975
3. Schneider, F, et al. 'Subcortical Correlates of Differential
    Classical Conditioning of Adversive Emotional Reactions
    in Social Phobia', *Journal of Biological Psychiatry*, 1999,
    45:863–71

Take Off Your Mud-coloured Spectacles

1. Rapee, RM, Heimberg RG. 'A Cognitive Behavioral
    Model of Anxiety in Social Phobia', *Journal of
    Behavioral Research Therapy*, 1997, 35:741–56

2. Zimbardo, PG. *Shyness, What it Is, What to Do About it*, Reading, Massachusetts, 1977
3. Ibid.
4. Vasey, M, Crnic, KA, Carter, WG. 'Worry In Childhood: A Developmental Perspective', *Cognitive Therapy Research*, 1994, 18:529–49
5. Fehm, L, Margraf, J. 'Thought Suppression: Specificity in Agoraphobia Versus Broad Impairment In Social Phobia', *Journal of Behavioral Research Therapy*, 2002, 40:57–66

Don't Be a Sucker for Rejection

1. Bukowsky, WM, Hoza, B, Boivin, M. 'Popularity, Friendship, and Emotional Adjustment During Early Adolescence', *New Directions in Child Development*, Summer 1993, 60:23–37

Come Back Down off the Ceiling

1. Stopa, L, Clark, DM. 'Social Phobia and the Interpretation of Social Events', *Journal of Behavioral Research Therapy*, 2000, 38:273–83
2. Ibid.
3. Ibid.
4. Rapee, RM. 'Perceived Threat and Perceived Control as Predictors of the Degree of Fear in Physical and Social Situations', *Journal of Anxiety Disorders*, 1997, 11:455–61

Slay the Monster Memories

1. Fehm, L, Margraf, J. 'Thought Suppression: Specificity in Agoraphobia Versus Broad Impairment in Social Phobia?', *Journal of Behavioral Research Therapy*, 2002, 40:57–66

2. Roebers, CM, Wuerzburg, U, Schneider, W. 'Individual Differences in Children's Eyewitness Recall: the Influence of Intelligence and Shyness', *Applied Developmental Science*, 2001, 5(1):9–20

3. Rachman, S, Gruter-Andrew, J, Shafran, R. 'Post Event Processing in Social Anxiety', *Journal of Behavioral Research Therapy*, 2000, 38:611–7

4. Mattick, RP, Page, AC, Lampe, L. 'Cognitive and Behavioral Aspects' in Stein, MB (Ed.), *Social Phobia: Clinical and Research Perspectives*, American Psychiatric Press, Inc, Washington DC, 1995

I Think I'm Beginning to Love You, Self

1. Pilkonis, PA, Heape, C, Klein, RH. 'Treating Shyness and Other Psychiatric Difficulties in Psychiatric Outpatients', *Communication Education*, 1980, 29:250–5

Who's the Boss? Your Mind or Body?

1. Festinger, LA. *Theory of Cognitive Dissonance*, Stanford University Press, Stanford, CA, 1957

2. Aronson, E. 'A Theory of Cognitive Dissonance', *American Journal of Psychology*, Spring 1997, 110(1):127–37

Snobs Don't Smile Either

1. Berent, JACSW. *Beyond Shyness*, Simon & Schuster, New York, 1993

2. Markway, BG, PhD, Carmin, CN, PhD, Pollard CA, PhD, Flynn, T, PhD. *Dying of Embarrassment*, New Harbinger Publications Inc., Oakland, CA, 1992

Battling Blushing, Sweating, and Clammy Hands
1. Amies, PL, Gelder, ML, Shaw, PM. 'Social Phobia: a Comparative Clinical Study', *British Journal of Psychiatry*, February 1983, 142:174–9

The Power and Pleasure of Anonymity
1. Zimbardo, PG. *Shyness, What it Is, What to Do About it*, Perseus Books, Reading, MA, 1977

The Shy's Sneaky Way to Get a Super Job
1. Capsi, A, Elder, GH, Bern, DJ. 'Moving away from the World: Life-course Patterns of Shy Children', *Journal of Developmental Psychology*, 1988, 24:824–31
2. Hamer, RJ, Bruch, MA. 'Personality Factors and Inhibited Career Development: Testing the Unique Contribution of Shyness', *Journal of Vocational Behavior*, 1997, 50:382–400

Going to a Party Is Not 'Going to a Party'
1. Wells A, Clark DM, Salovskis P, et al. 'Social Phobia: The Role of In-situation Safety Behaviors in Maintaining Anxiety and Negative Beliefs', *Journal of Behavioral Therapy*, 1995, 26:153–61
2. Ibid.

Getting Legless Is Not the Answer
1. Otto, MR, et al. 'Alcohol Dependence in Panic Disorder Patients', *Journal of Psychiatric Research*, 1992, 26:29–38
2. Shucket, MA. 'Genetic and Clinical Implications of Alcohol and Affective Disorder', *American Journal of Psychiatry*, 1986, 143:9:140–7

3. Schneier, FR, et al. 'Alcohol Abuse and Social Phobia', *Journal of Anxiety Disorders*, 1989, 3:15–23

The Danger of Being a Denying Shy
1. Schneier, Franklin, MD, Welkowitz, L, PhD. *The Hidden Face of Shyness*, Avon Books, New York, 1996

The Proven Eye-contact Cure
1. Bald, M. 'Organizing the Shy: VVM, the Association of Shy People in the Netherlands', *World Press Review*, November 1998
2. Silverman, LK. 'Parenting Young Gifted Children', in Whitmore, JR (Ed.), *Intellectual Giftedness in Young Children*, The Haworth Press, New York, 1986
3. Kellerman, J, et al. 'Looking and Loving: The Effects of Mutual Gaze on Feelings of Romantic Love', *Journal of Research in Personality*, 1989, 23(2):145–61

Chameleons Should Choose Their Colours Carefully
1. Bukowsky, WM, Hoza, B, Boivin, M. 'Popularity, Friendship, and Emotional Adjustment During Early Adolescence', *New Directions in Child Development*, Summer 1993, 60:23–37
2. Taylor, AR. 'Predictors of Peer Rejection in Early Elementary Grades: Roles of Problem Behavior, Academic Achievement, and Teacher Preference', *Journal of Clinical Child Psychology*, 1989, 18:360–5

Social Blooper Remedy

1. Dayhoff, SA, PhD. *Diagonally-parked in a Parallel Universe,* Effectiveness-Plus Publications, Placitas, NM, 2000
2. Carducci, BJ, PhD. *Shyness, a Bold New Approach*, HarperCollins, New York, 1999
3. Martin, J. *Miss Manners' Guide for the Turn-of-the-Millennium*, Fireside, New York, 1990
4. Asher, J. *Psychology Today*, reporting on studies by Stephen J. Suomi at the National Institute of Child Health and Human Development in Bethesda, MD, April 1987

There Are No Love 'Guarantees'

1. Berent, JACSW. *Beyond Shyness,* Simon & Schuster, New York, 1993

Oversexed or Underconfident

1. Dayhoff, SA, PhD. *Diagonally-parked in a Parallel Universe*, Effectiveness-Plus Publications, Placitas, NM, 2000
2. Carducci, BJ, PhD. *Shyness, a Bold New Approach*, HarperCollins, New York, 1999
3. Zimbardo, PG. *Shyness, What it Is, What to Do About it,* Perseus Books, Reading, MA, 1977

Relationship Rehearsals

1. Walster, E, Walster, WG, and Berscheid, E. *Equity: Theory and Research*, Allyn and Bacon, Boston, 1978

The Lovin' Is Easy. It's the Getting There That's Hard

1. Cooper PJ, Eke M. 'Childhood Shyness and Maternal Social Phobia: a Community Study', *British Journal of Psychiatry*, 1999, 174:439–43
2. Alden, L, Cappe, R. 'Interpersonal Process Training for Shy Clients' in Jones, WH, Cheek, JM, Briggs, SR (Eds), *Shyness: Perspectives on Research and Treatment*, Plenum, New York, 1986

Shall I Put on a Big Act?

1. Oguchi, T, et al. 'Voice and Interpersonal Attraction', *Japanese Psychological Research*, March 1997, 39(1):56–61
2. Zimbardo, PG. *Shyness, What it Is, What to Do About it*, Perseus Books, Reading, MA, 1977
3. Ibid.

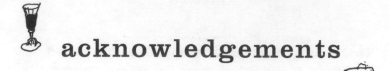

acknowledgements

I am very grateful to the following people who openly shared stories of their shyness ordeals with me. And also to those who e-mailed me after the publication of this book. Thank you from the bottom of my heart.

Alexandra T., Alexia P., Aliia P., Alisa L., Alison M., Allison D., Alvin V., Amanda G., Amanda P., Amanda R., Amber T., Amy P., Andrew D., Andy H., Angela B., Anna E., Antony T., Ariana G., Babs J., Barb G., Ben K., Beth P., Bob I., Boris P., Brigette S., Brittany V., Bruce P., Buddy K., Burt F., Candace L., Candy G., Carrie B., Chelsea W., Cheryl M., Chris O., Chris T., Chris U., Claire F., Coral B., Courtney U., Curt H., Dalton H., Dan Y., Dana J., Daniel T., Danielle L., Darla P., Darlene D., Dave B., Dave F., Dean P., Deeana P., Denise D., Diana L., Diana P., Diane F., Diane M., Dimitri D., Don M., Donna I., Donna J., Doug S., Drew P., Dusty P., Eric P., Fanny T., Felicia G., Felicia H., Fred P., Gail F., Gail H., Gatsah W., Geoffrey F., Greg L., Greg. P., Haley U., Hannah R., Holly K., Holly P., Ian H., Jacques C., James S., Jean S., Jeannie D., Jennie H., Jeremy D., Joanie B., John P., John R., Jolene Q., Julia S., Kahya V., Karen J., Katelyn B., Katherine I., Katrina A., Kayla U., Keil W., Kelley P., Ken L., Kendra G., Kendra S., Kerrie G., Kevin N., Kevin O., Kimberly E., Koos Z., Lamont F., Laura F., Laurel L., Lenore P., Leslie K., Linda G., Lindsey L., Liod W., Lisa E., Llani U., Lucas H., Luigi A., Marcia S., Mark J., Mark M., Mark S., Matthew W., Megan P., Megan Y., Meredith A., Meryl M., Michael K., Michael T., Mike B., Moishe R., Nathan F., Nathan K., Nicole G., Nicole S., Nikhil B., Olgatina P., Pam L., Pamela U., Paul M., Paula K., Pennant I., Phil P., Phillip T., Rachel G., Rachel T., Rafael J., Ralph O., Renee H., Richard K., Riki D., Robert Y., Ron W., Ron P., Ron M., Ronald J., Samuel Y., Sandra M., Sandra T., Sandy C., Scott P., Sean L., Sebastian F., Shannon A., Shav R., Shawn D., Shelley H., Shelly T., Sonja P., Stephen O., Steve C., Steve N., Steve S., Sukumar S., Sussana A., Suzanne Y., Syafique S., Terry H., Thabiet S., Tina P., Tom A., Tony S., Tony V., Travis O., Troy T., Tyler C., Tyler H., Vanessa C., Vicky A., Victoria T., Vincent A., Wesley P., Will K.